THE SALESPERSON'S LEGAL GUIDE

Steven Mitchell Sack & Howard Jay Steinberg

Prentice-Hall, Inc., Englewood Cliffs, New Jersey

The *Salesperson's Legal Guide*
by Steven Mitchell Sack and Howard Jay Steinberg

Printed in the United States of America

Prentice-Hall International, Inc., London/Prentice-Hall of Australia, Pty. Ltd., Sydney/Prentice-Hall of Canada, Ltd., Toronto/Prentice-Hall of India Private Ltd., New Delhi/Prentice-Hall of Japan, Inc., Tokyo/Prentice-Hall of Southeast Asia Pt. Ltd., Singapore/Whitehall Books Limited, Wellington, New Zealand

10 9 8 7 6 5 4 3 2 1

Library of Congress Cataloging in Publication Data

Sack, Steven Mitchell, date
  The salesperson's legal guide.

  Includes index.
    1. Sales personnel—Legal status, laws, etc.—
United States. 2. Labor contract—United States.
3. Sales personnel—Salaries, commissions, etc.—
United States. I. Steinberg, Howard Jay, date
joint author. II. Title.
KF3580.R3S2   344.73'0176165885   80-22647
ISBN 0-13-788190-8
ISBN 0-13-788182-7 (pbk.)

To our parents, grandparents, and the ambassadors of industry who beat a loud drum.

Foreword

This book can save you money and aggravation.

If you are a salesperson, this book will tell you how to protect your interests. It will inform you of your legal rights and remedies during all stages of the employment relationship—before, during, and even after your employment status with a particular company has ended. You will learn what to do when a dispute arises with your company. After reading this book, you will have a better understanding of knowing when your company did something wrong and what you can do about it.

There are presently millions of salespeople working in the United States who earn their livelihood in a variety of selling specialties. They include furniture, gift, mass marketing, industrial, retail salesmen, and a multitude of others. Often they sign contracts prepared by the legal staffs of their employers. These contracts are slanted for the benefit of the company, and most salesmen are unaware of the pitfalls of such contracts or unable to appraise them.

Many salespeople, unfortunately, think they "know it all" and do not wish to invest the time to learn about their legal rights. These people are often exploited by their companies. Their commissions may be withheld without their even knowing it. However, salespeople who wish to learn about their rights will profit. Opportunities for literally millions of dollars a year arising from potential lawsuits are squandered by salesmen who are unaware that they have legally justifiable claims.

This book is *not* meant to replace a lawyer. It cannot definitively answer all legal questions concerning the relationship with your employer, since disputes are usually resolved by analyzing the law in a state as it relates to the unique facts of each case. However, these materials contain practical, useful information about the law of contracts that can be used to a salesman's advantage. For example, in addition to discussing beneficial provisions that should be included in the contracts salesmen sign, you will learn what clauses favor the company and how these can be modified to better your interests. All provisions are explained so that you will have a better understanding of how they are used.

If you have an oral contract with your employer, you will find information revealing how your employment status can be substantially improved and protected. In short, whether you are a novice salesman or an experienced pro, you will become more informed and less vulnerable to being subjected to the injustices of your trade.

It is hoped that no one will sit down and try to read the book straight through. Even though it has been specifically written for lay people and assumes that the reader has little, if any, formal knowledge of the law, it should be read carefully without trying to absorb too much of the material at one time in order to obtain its maximum benefits.

We believe that such a work could not have been written at a more appropriate time. Salesmen in all industries are currently organizing to obtain rights that they feel they deserve. There was an effort to secure increased benefits through the Sales Representative's Protection Act in 1976. Unfortunately, this attempt was unsuccessful, thus continuing to leave the salesman's fate in his own hands.

Our book has been written to alleviate this need. It is designed to prevent the salesman from being continuously abused because of lack of knowledge of the law. This is our attempt to "sell a salesman," and we are certain that this book will be a valuable resource.

Steven Mitchell Sack, Esq.
Howard Jay Steinberg, Esq.

Contents

Foreword   iv

1. TERMS OF EMPLOYMENT   1

Section 1 Oral Contracts of Employment   2
Section 2 Written Contracts of Employment   7
Section 3 Determining the Status of the Salesman   15

2. COMMISSION SALESMEN   18

Section 4 Commissions   18
Section 5 Territorial Rights   35
Section 6 Proper Accounting   39

3. COMPETING WITH YOUR COMPANY   43

Section 7 Duties of the Salesman   43
Section 8 Restrictive Covenants in Employment
          Contracts   46

4. CHANGING YOUR CONTRACTUAL
       RELATIONSHIP   51

Section 9 Modification of the Contract   51
Section 10 Rescission of the Contract   56

5. REMEDIES FOR BREACH OF CONTRACT   62

Section 11   Breach of Contract   62
Section 12   Unjust Enrichment   71

6. THE SALESMAN'S LEGAL OPTIONS   74

Section 13   Disputes With the Company   74
Section 14   Out-of-Court Settlements   76
Section 15   Arbitration   79
Section 16   Small Claims Court   84
Section 17   Litigation   90

7. PROTECTING THE SALESMAN FROM EXPLOITATION   94

Section 18   Job Misrepresentation   94
Section 19   Protecting Your Money-Making Ideas   97
Section 20   Inconveniences While "On the Road"   98
Section 21   The Company Goes Bankrupt   103

8. TAX TIPS FOR THE SALESMAN   109

Conclusion   124
Glossary of Terms   126
Index   131

Acknowledgments

Special thanks are given to Ellen Slater, who spent countless hours typing our manuscript. In addition, we would like to thank the Bureau of Wholesale Sales Representatives, Atlanta, Georgia, for permitting us to include excerpts of its Standard Salesman's Contract for illustrative purposes. We also express our gratitude to the Lawyers Co-Operative Publishing Co., which allowed us to include excerpts from material contained in *American Jurisprudence Legal Forms*, and to Gerald Nissenbaum, Esq., of Boston, Massachusetts, for his helpful suggestions.

Finally, the authors wish to express their gratitude to Bernard Sack, salesman *par excellence*, whose determination, insight, and assistance made this book a reality.

Authors' Note

The information contained in this book is the result of in-depth research into legal problems that salespeople generally encounter. Individual fact situations cannot be anticipated. Therefore, if you have any questions regarding the applicability of any of the helpful hints contained in this book, you should consult an attorney, accountant, or other professional.

It is additionally recognized, of course, that women engage in selling occupations. However, for the sake of convenience, we refer to all salespersons as "salesmen." Be assured that no offense is intended.

1

TERMS OF EMPLOYMENT

This first chapter will examine various contractual arrangements that salesmen have with their companies. In addition, it will offer suggestions as to how salesmen can protect themselves when disputes arise.

The federal government has passed a number of laws to protect a person regardless of the terms of his contract. Among these federal laws are statutes that provide that a salesman cannot be fired because of: (1) race, color, religion, sex, or national origin; (2) age; (3) debt; (4) union organization activities; or (5) for invoking the protections of the Fair Labor Standards Act.

There are also state laws that protect you. If you believe you have been fired or discriminated against for any of the above reasons, you should contact the appropriate state or federal agency *immediately*. If you delay, you may lose your chance to sue. Many of these laws require that you file a complaint within a limited number of days after your discharge from the company.

Unfortunately, federal and state laws offer only limited protection. The following sections will teach you how to fully protect your interests.

SECTION 1
ORAL CONTRACTS OF EMPLOYMENT

A. WHAT IS AN ORAL CONTRACT?

An oral contract is a verbal agreement between the salesman and his company defining their working relationship. These contracts are usually binding if the duties, compensation, and terms of employment are agreed upon by both parties.

Salesmen often have oral agreements because their companies refuse to give them a written contract. Many companies like to use oral contracts because there is no written evidence to indicate what terms were prepared and accepted by both parties when they entered into their employment arrangement. If disputes arise, it is more difficult for the salesman to prove that the company failed to abide by the terms of the agreement. For example, if a 6 percent commission rate was accepted orally, a dishonest employer could deny this by stating that a lower commission rate had been accepted. The salesman would then have to prove that both parties had agreed upon the higher commission figure.

When a legal dispute arises concerning the terms of an oral contract, a court will resolve the problem by examining all the evidence that the salesman and company offer and weighing the testimony to determine who is telling the truth.

B. PROTECTIVE MEASURES

All salesmen should try to obtain a written contract. However, if your company refuses to sign a written agreement, there are various ways to protect yourself if you have an oral contract. Your chief concern should be directed toward obtaining written evidence that indicates the accepted terms, including information that defines your commission rate, the assigned territory, compensation for traveling expenses, etc.

If your company refuses to sign a written contract, it is advisable to write letters to the company whenever you reach an oral agreement relating to your job. For instance, if you orally agree to sell certain products at a 10 percent commission rate for a period of one year, you should send a certified letter to the company similar to the following:

ABC Enterprises, Inc.   Date _____
Main Street
Anywhere, U.S.A.
c/o Mr. John Doe, President of Sales

Dear John,

I enjoyed meeting with you on (date) and look forward to working with you. It is my understanding that we have agreed that I will sell (name of products or services to be provided) at the rate of 10 percent commission for a term of one year starting (date). It is also understood that I will be the exclusive selling agent in the (territory) and will be reimbursed for (expenses agreed upon).

If this letter is substantially accurate, I would appreciate if you would sign the enclosed copy and return it to me. I expect to hear from you shortly.

Sincerely,
Stuart Salesman

Company by _____
Title _____
Dated _____

Be as specific as possible when referring to subjects that you and the company have agreed upon. Write the letter with precision, since ambiguous terms are resolved *against* the letter writer. Be sure to keep a copy of the letter for your own records and, if possible, have a representative of the company sign a copy and return it to you.

If, at a later date, the terms of the oral agreement are changed (for instance, additional territory is assigned to you), write another letter specifying the new arrangement that has been reached. Keep a copy of this letter and *all* correspondence sent to and received from your company.

If your company does not notify you that the terms specified in your letter are incorrect, this letter will serve as valuable evidence should you later need to prove the terms of your agreement. Some courts have stated that the company's failure to respond indicated that the terms specified in the letter were the terms actually agreed upon.

Once the company writes you a letter that states the terms of the oral agreement, the letter can be used as evidence to prove the terms of your employment. However, if the company does not wish to write such a letter, it is best if they indicate in writing some of the terms that have been agreed upon. For instance, if you receive a 10 percent commission rate and have sold $10,000 worth of goods, have your employer note on your check, "$1,000 paid based on $10,000 sales." The agreed-upon commission rate can then be determined by simple arithmetic should a dispute arise in the future.

C. UNENFORCEABLE ORAL CONTRACTS

You are under no legal duty to follow the terms of an unenforceable contract. Oral contracts will generally not be enforced by the courts if the terms of the contract are to last longer than one year. This arises from legal principles based upon the Statute of Frauds. The Statute of Frauds is a rule of law requiring that certain contracts be in writing to be enforceable. Thus, if you orally agreed to work for your company for two years, either you or the company could terminate the relationship prior to two years without penalty. And, an oral agreement not to compete with your employer for five years after you leave the company would not be enforceable due to the Statute of Frauds.

However, if it is possible that the terms of your agreement can be performed within one year, the oral agreement will be binding. For instance, if you are orally hired *at will* (see next section for a definition) and work seven years for the company, the contract will be enforceable in court, since you could have been terminated during the first year of your employment.

It is possible to have an *enforceable* oral agreement extending beyond one year if you receive a memorandum or letter that states:

1. The names of the salesman and company;
2. The duties of the salesman and the terms that have been agreed upon; and
3. The manner in which you will be paid.

This information can be either contained in one letter or pieced together from separate writings. However, these memoranda or letters *must* be signed or initialed by your employer. A small number of states require both the salesman and a company official to sign the letters.

If you have a contract that is part oral and part written, most states view the agreement as an oral contract. Thus, if you had a written agreement that specified a 3 percent rate of commission and had an oral agreement that you would be employed for five years, the entire agreement may be viewed as an oral contract and may not be legally binding because it called for performance in excess of one year.

D. OFFERS OF EMPLOYMENT VIA TELEPHONE

Salesmen are often hired as a result of telephone conversations with company officials. These arrangements sometimes occur when the salesman is attempting to obtain a sideline to supplement his income. Such business agreements made via the telephone should be entered into with great caution.

Many salesmen have been victimized by unscrupulous companies in the past. For example, after agreeing to terms and investing time and money selling goods for the company, a salesman may be told that the person who offered him a specified commission rate did not have the authority to bind the company and was no longer working there. On other occasions salesmen have been told to "show us what you can do and write your own ticket" only to find stiff opposition from the company once their orders have been placed. These abuses need not occur and can be prevented by the following simple steps:

1. *Always* find out whom you are talking with, what his position is, and the extent of his authority to bind the company;

2. Before you begin working, write a letter that includes all of the terms that have been agreed upon. Have a copy signed by a company official and returned to you;

3. Do *not* rely on promises that terms will be worked out at a later date;

4. If you are unfamiliar with the company, ask for the names of a few customers who are currently being shipped products or receive services. Call them to obtain information about the company;

5. Learn who previously represented the company and why they are no longer in that position. Then talk to the former salesperson.

These measures will not ensure that your relationship with the company will be a smooth one, but they do provide you with some protection and a basis for legal action should problems later develop.

Helpful Hints
If you have an oral contract, do not forget to:

1. Either ask for or send a letter to the company by certified mail that states the *precise* terms that have been agreed upon. You should always include your name and the name of the company, the commission rate, territory assignment, terms of employment, and method of compensation. Attempt to get your employer to sign this letter.

2. *Never* rely on a company's promise to work out terms at a later date.

3. Keep records of *all* correspondence and payments.

SECTION 2
WRITTEN CONTRACTS OF EMPLOYMENT

A. EMPLOYMENT AT WILL CONTRACTS

1. What Is Employment at Will?

An employment at will provision in a contract provides that you can be fired or resign for a good reason, a bad reason, or no reason at all. Many salesmen have this type of work arrangement with their employers. The following is an example of such a clause in a contract:

> Either party shall have the right to terminate this agreement prior to the expiration of the term provided written notice of intention to terminate is given the other party at least sixty days prior to the expiration of the term.

According to the terms of this provision, your company could fire you as long as it gave sixty days' written notice. If you have an *oral* contract with your company, the law presumes that your relationship is terminable at will unless there are circumstances that clearly indicate that both parties intended otherwise.

2. Common Areas of Confusion

Many salesmen who are hired at will have the mistaken belief that they were hired for a one-year period. This confusion can be illustrated by use of the following types of clauses:

a. Compensation rates defined in annual terms
The following is an example of such a clause:

Salesman will work at the rate of $X annually.

This does not mean that the contract has a one-year term and that you cannot be fired before a year has expired. Such language merely fixes the rate of the salesman's pay and does not provide for the length of his employment.

b. Territorial rights stated in annual terms

The fact that a salesman is assigned a territory for a specific period of time does not prevent him from being fired before that time period has expired. An example of such a clause follows:

> Your assignment in X county will continue for a period of twelve months.

Courts usually interpret this to mean that the time period stated in the contract merely indicates how long the expected territorial assignment will last. They will not allow such a provision to convert a terminable at will employment relationship into a contract of a specific duration.

3. Protection for the Salesman

Very few restrictions are placed upon a company that seeks to terminate an employment at will contractual relationship. However, a salesman's termination cannot result from bad faith, malice, or be based upon retaliation. For example, if your company fires you to free itself from paying commissions that will become due, this would be considered conduct motivated by bad faith according to the law in several states. However, this bad-faith rule is not universally accepted and is very hard to prove in court. If you are fired because you have an argument with a supervisor, or the boss does not like the color of your tie, or even if no reason is given, chances are you will have no legal recourse. This is the disadvantage of an employment at will contract, and all salesmen should avoid working pursuant to this arrangement whenever possible.

Many salesmen believe it is advantageous to have an employment at will contract because they can change jobs whenever they desire; for example, when goods are not being delivered, or they do not receive proper accounting. However, salesmen can leave the employ of the company under these circumstances even when hired for a specific term. The company's failure to perform important terms of the contract will generally allow the salesman to terminate his employment regardless of the terms.

Remember, if you can be fired or resign anytime, you have been hired at will. Since employment at will contracts offer little job security, salesmen need protection. The following types of clauses may be helpful:

a. Guaranteed sales quota

This provision guarantees your job as long as your sales remain above a certain level. An example of such a provision states:

> The Company agrees that the Sales Representative will continue to represent it as long as his total volume of sales maintains a minimum level of $X per calendar quarter.

b. Seasonal guarantee

If your product is seasonal, you should also seek a clause that protects you from being fired in the middle of a selling season. For instance:

> This contract may be canceled by either party upon ninety days' written notice to the other party. However, in no event shall any such notice of cancellation be effective until the end of the selling season during which said notice is given.

Both of these clauses will increase your job security and are compromises that many companies will accept.

B. NOTICE OF TERMINATION

1. What Is a Notice of Termination?

A notice of termination is usually a written letter indicating that your services are no longer required by the company, and the company is usually required to notify the salesman a specified number of days in advance of termination. Frequently both the salesman and his company have the option of deciding whether or not to terminate by written notice. An example of such a provision follows:

> *Either party may cancel and terminate this agreement at any time by giving the other party sixty days' written notice. This will be delivered personally or by prepaid certified letter directed to the last known address of the party to be affected by such notice, and the notice shall be deemed effective from the date said certified letter is deposited in the post office.*

Under the terms of this clause, the contract would be terminated sixty days after the letter was deposited at the post office.

2. What Happens When the Company Gives Improper Notice?

A common problem arises when a salesman is discharged without receiving written notice, or the salesman is given shorter written notice than the time period stated in the contract. For example, written notice of termination is given to the salesman ten days prior to termination instead of sixty days as stated in his contract. If this occurs, the salesman will still be discharged and his damages are limited to the compensation that he would have earned during the notice period. Thus, if a salesman was fired with thirty days' notice and his contract called for sixty days' notice, he would only be entitled to collect damages for what his salary and commissions would have been for the next thirty days. His term of employment does not continue to run indefinitely if proper notice is not given.

If a salesman's contract calls for written notice and none is given by the company, some courts have ruled that the employment arrangement and company obligations continue until the salesman receives written notice as specified in his contract. However, most courts limit the salesman's damages to the notice period specified in the contract

3. **Compensation for the Salesman Despite Proper Notice**

There are circumstances when a salesman will be entitled to continued compensation despite the fact that he received *proper* notice of termination.

a. Money that becomes due after termination

If a salesman was an important factor in obtaining a sale that was concluded after he was terminated, many courts have ruled that he would be entitled to collect tne commissions from the sale despite the fact that he was fired. His termination will not result in his losing the right to those commissions.

b. Opportunity for corrective action

Some clauses provide that if a salesman fails to perform his obligations—for example, if his sales quota falls below a certain level—he can take corrective action before he is terminated. The following is an example of such a provision:

> *In the event of default or breach of the provisions by either party, the party not at fault shall give to the defaulting party sixty days' written notice of claim of default and intention to cancel the contract, specifying the particular breach that has been made. Unless this breach is corrected within sixty days, the party serving such notice may, if the breach actually existed, cancel and terminate the contract.*

This clause is quite beneficial. With this provision, the notice of termination must state how your performance was deficient. You are then given a certain time period to take corrective action. In the above example you would have sixty days to raise your sales to the expected quota. If you were merely given written notice of termination and this did not state the reasons *why* your job was being terminated, such notice would not terminate your contract. You would be entitled to damages beyond the sixty-day period specified in the contract.

4. Losing Your Right to Notice

Under certain circumstances, the company is not obligated to give you a notice of termination notwithstanding the fact that your contract says so. This will occur if you fail to perform certain important obligations. For example, in one case a salesman failed to solicit sales and purchase supplies. The court ruled that the salesman had breached important duties of his contract and the company was not liable for damages when they fired him without notice.

C. GOOD-CAUSE PROVISIONS

1. What Is Good Cause?

A provision in a contract that states that the salesman will be terminated only for good cause protects the salesman if he is fired. The following is an example of such a provision:

> It is agreed that the work of the Selling Representative will be of a permanent nature and the Representative will hold the position as long as the Representative is, in the Company's opinion, efficient, conscientious, and productive. If he is not, it remains within the discretion of the Company to relieve the Representative of his employment by the full payment of whatever is owed Representative at the time of such termination.

There are many good-cause reasons that justify a salesman's termination. They include neglect of duty; negligence; incompetence; dishonesty; intoxication; disobedience of the company's rules, instructions, or orders; insolence, disrespect, and unbecoming conduct; and unfaithfulness to the company's interests.

Your company must use good faith in exercising its discretion to terminate the contract if you have such a provision. However, if your company has good cause to terminate you, it can do so without incurring a penalty even though your contract may be for a definite period of time that has not yet expired.

2. Advantages of Good-Cause Provisions

These provisions are usually found in contracts where the salesman is hired for a definite, specified term (for example, one year). The words "good cause" do not have to be included in the language of the provision. If the salesman is fired, the company must prove that it had reasonable grounds for the termination. If it fails to provide an adequate explanation for such actions, the company will be in breach of contract and will be liable for damages.

If you have a provision of this type, you cannot be fired arbitrarily. You will be able to work for the time period specified in the contract and cannot be terminated because of so-called changes in company policy. In short, this provision enhances your job security.

D. HIRED FOR A SPECIFIED DURATION

These contracts provide that the salesman will be hired for a specific period of time. An example of such a provision follows:

> *The Company agrees to hire the Salesman for a period of one (1) year commencing on January 1, 1981, and lasting through December 31, 1981. This contract shall be renewed from year to year at the option of either party by mailing written notice of intention to renew thirty (30) days prior to the termination date.*

Even with this provision, a salesman may be terminated prior to the specified period if the company has good cause to fire him (see preceding section).

If you have a contract that provides that you will be hired for a fixed period of time and you continue working for the company beyond the stated period without entering into a new agreement, it is generally presumed that the old contract has been *renewed* for the same fixed period of time. For example, a two-year contract would be viewed as being renewed for an additional two years.

E. PERMANENT OR LIFETIME CONTRACTS

1. What Is a Lifetime Contract?

A lifetime employment contract arises when the salesman is guaranteed a position with the company for as long as he lives. Unfortunately for the salesman, courts are generally reluctant to view a contract as creating permanent or lifetime employment. Usually, such contracts are viewed as being terminable at will by either party. Thus, a "lifetime contract" may theoretically be terminated after one day.

A valid lifetime contract is very hard to obtain. Even the president of the company does not have the authority to bind the corporation by offering you a lifetime contract. Furthermore, some states have laws that limit the duration of an employment contract to a specified number of years. This would prevent you from having an enforceable lifetime contract.

2. Obtaining an Enforceable Lifetime Contract

If you are able to obtain a lifetime employment contract, the best way to ensure that the courts *may* uphold this agreement is to:

a. Have the managing Board of Directors of the corporation clearly indicate in the contract that it is offering you lifetime employment. However, even the Board of Directors may not have the authority to grant you such a contract.

b. Have the contract include language such as ". . . for the life of the Selling Agent" or ". . . for as long as the Salesman is physically able to work." It is not advisable to use the phrase "permanent employment" unless additional language is included to clarify the intentions of both you and your company. Courts generally interpret "permanent employment" to mean steady employment, not lifetime employment.

c. Give something of value to the company. Courts usually require a salesman to relinquish something of value other than his promise to work for the company. Such examples of valuable contributions to the company include:

1. Money or property that you may contribute to the business;

2. Surrendering a claim for money that the company owes you; or

3. Reducing your salary and/or other benefits.

The relinquishment of another job, business, or profession in order to accept a contract of lifetime employment is generally not viewed as being sufficient to make the contract binding. Thus, if you currently have a contract that you believe is for lifetime employment, it may not be enforceable. Consult an attorney if you hope to obtain such a contract in the future.

SECTION 3
DETERMINING THE STATUS OF THE SALESMAN

Salesmen are usually placed into two broad categories with respect to their employment status. They are considered either employees or independent selling agents and it is important to realize the distinction between these two classifications. A saleman who is an employee of a company is entitled to far more benefits than a salesman who is considered to be an independent selling agent. Independent agents are:

1. Not covered by Workmen's Compensation;

2. Not covered by unemployment insurance;

3. Not protected by the National Labor Relations Act, which provides benefits to organized labor;

4. Not entitled to FICA contributions from their companies; and

5. Not usually entitled to participate in group, life, and health plans, profit sharing, and medical reimbursement plans.

If your company considers you to be an independent selling agent, that does not necessarily mean that you are one.

Attempt to have the following provision inserted in your contract to ensure that you will be treated as an employee:

> *The Company agrees that for the purpose of the Federal Insurance Contributions Act and the applicable State Workmen's Compensation and Unemployment Compensation Acts, the Salesman shall be considered an employee and covered under such acts.*

A. ARE YOU AN INDEPENDENT SELLING AGENT?

There is no precise legal definition that explains what an independent selling agent is. When the courts attempt to determine whether a salesman is an independent selling agent, they analyze the facts of the particular salesman's case. The most significant factors that courts look at when making this determination are:

1. The company's right of control over the salesman;

2. Whether or not the company carries indemnity or liability insurance on the salesman;

3. Whether or not the salesman is included in Workmen's Compensation coverage;

4. Whether or not the company withholds federal income taxes and takes Social Security deductions from the salesman's pay.

Even if the company does *not* carry insurance, Workmen's Compensation coverage, or contribute FICA taxes for the salesman, he may still be an employee of the company. The *most* significant factor in determining employee status is the company's right to control the duties and functions of the salesman.

The company's right to control is best explained by the use of examples. Courts have found salesmen to be employees if their companies:

1. Had the right to supervise the details of their operations;

2. Required the salesman to collect accounts on behalf of the company;

3. Provided him with a company car and/or reimbursement for some or all expenses;

4. Restricted his ability to carry other lines or work for other companies;

5. Required him to call on particular customers;

6. Provided him with insurance or Workmen's Compensation benefits; and

7. Deducted income and Social Security FICA taxes.

This list is not meant to be all-inclusive. These factors are merely listed to help you realize whether there is a possibility that the law treats you as an employee of your company. Remember, even though your job description is that of a "sales agent" or "independent selling representative," you may nevertheless be an employee.

B. BENEFITS OF EMPLOYEE STATUS

Companies classify you as an independent selling agent because they do not have to pay for your benefits. If you press your company to provide you with employee benefits, you may be terminated, particularly if you have an employment at will contract. However, in certain instances it is beneficial to argue that you are an employee. For instance, if you are fired, seriously injured, or if your company goes out of business, you should consult an attorney in order to determine if you are eligible for benefits that an employee would normally receive. When a court or state agency determines that you are an employee, you may be able to gain:

1. Unemployment compensation if you are terminated;

2. Workmen's Compensation if you are injured;

3. FICA contributions on your behalf; and

4. An order of relief from a labor board depending upon the reasons why you were terminated.

2

COMMISSION SALESMEN

SECTION 4
COMMISSIONS

A. WHAT ARE COMMISSIONS?

Commissions are the rate of compensation paid to a salesman based upon a specified percentage of the gross or net sales received by his company. Gross sales are the total value of all placed orders. To arrive at a net sales figure, various items are deducted. For example, customers of the company are often able to reduce (that is, discount) their billings if they pay their bills by a specified date. Other items that reduce gross sales include returns, lower rates for off-price goods, freight charges, charge backs, bad debts, and advertising allowances. These are subtracted from the gross sales to arrive at a net sales figure upon which the salesman's commissions are based.

B. HOW COMMISSIONS ARE EARNED

1. By Accepted Orders
Generally, salesmen's commissions are earned when orders are received and accepted by the company. Language indicating this arrangement typically states the following:

The Company agrees to pay the Salesman as compensation for his services a commission of 8 percent on the net amount of sales made by the Salesman. Any order solicited, tendered, or otherwise obtained by the Salesman shall be forwarded to the Company for acceptance. The Company shall have the option of accepting or rejecting any orders taken by the Salesman, and all orders are subject to the Company's written acceptance. The Company reserves the absolute right to refuse acceptance.

Be aware of the presence of an "absolute discretion" provision (the last sentence). The company cannot reject your orders unless they have a valid business reason to do so, and courts will not allow a company to arbitrarily refuse to accept your orders. Thus, protest any indiscriminate rejections. However, if the account is going bankrupt, has a poor credit rating, is a slow payer, or you incorrectly quoted prices or delivery dates, this will justify the rejection of your orders.

2. By Shipped Orders

Many times the salesman will be unable to receive commissions except for goods actually shipped. The following provision indicates such an arrangement:

No commission shall be payable hereunder except on goods actually shipped by the Company and received and accepted by the purchaser.

Here, the salesman will *not* be entitled to commissions on sales made for goods that are *returned*. To avoid this situation, he should bargain for the right to receive full commissions *if credit* has been given for the returned goods.

If commissions are earned only after merchandise is shipped, the salesman is at the company's mercy to fill his orders. For a variety of reasons, a company may be unable to ship its goods at a rate that a salesman finds desirable. Thus, you need some guarantee that a specified percentage of your orders will be honored. *Insist* upon an 85 percent or more *guarantee clause* similar to the following:

> The Company guarantees to pay the Salesman commissions on a minimum of 85 percent of accepted orders, whether shipped or not. An order will be considered accepted unless the Company notifies the Salesman in writing, of any order or orders rejected, within fifteen days of the mailing of such orders by the Salesman. The Company guarantees to ship a minimum of 85 percent of accepted orders prior to the end of the delivery date specified on said order or orders. In the event that written notice of rejection is not given the Salesman within the time provided above, the Salesman shall become entitled to commissions on said 85 percent of all nonrejected, unshipped orders, which commissions shall be paid on the 15th day of the month following the last day of the season for which said order or orders were received by the Company.

This provision has been enforced by the courts in the past. They have stated that it is not unreasonable for a salesman to request and receive such a guarantee. A recent case declared that an 85 percent guaranteed commissions clause *would* protect the salesman in the event that a substantial degree of his efforts did not result in completed sales.

However, this clause does not give you an unlimited right to receive credit for all of the orders that you placed. You can only receive commissions on unshipped orders if the company's acceptance of orders in the aggregate are less than 85 percent. Also, remember that a company can nullify the advantage of this provision by promptly notifying you through the mail that your unshipped orders have been rejected. If this is done, you will be out of luck.

Helpful Hints
Some salesmen capitalize on the fact that companies often forget to mail these written rejections.

1. They keep a weekly list of all accepted and rejected orders;

2. Insist that all rejections be sent to them in writing; and

3. Send the company a letter that states they intend to enforce the 85 percent guarantee.

One salesman who followed these helpful hints recovered additional commissions. The court ruled that his orders were accepted when he did not receive a written letter within fifteen days notifying him of the rejection.

3. Impossibility of Performance

Although you have an 85 percent guarantee, it may not be enforced by a court, particularly when conditions make it impossible for the company to perform its obligations. This legal excuse is referred to as impossibility of performance and it occurs, for example, when the company's employees are on strike, there is a trade embargo or an energy crisis, or a fire at the company's plant makes the company unable to ship its goods.

If you are told not to sell company goods in the event of a labor strike or trade embargo, you may be unable to obtain commission on such unshipped goods even with your 85 percent guarantee. However, the company may still be responsible for producing, shipping, and honoring its contractual obligations if it was aware of these conditions but sent you out to procure orders anyway.

Helpful Hints

If you are paid on a salary plus commission basis, you want to make sure that your contract will not be terminated in the event that a fire destroys company property. Include a clause similar to the following to receive added protection:

> *This contract shall not be terminated, nor shall its obligations cease, by the temporary impairment of the business by fire which causes destruction of Company property, including but not limited to business and*

credit records, or commodities with which the Company deals. If the business is so impaired, the length of the employment term shall be extended for an equal period of time.

C. OFF-PRICE AND DISCOUNT GOODS

Off-price goods are goods sold by the company at a reduced rate. Salesmen frequently allow the company to decide whether commissions should be paid depending upon the price at which the goods are sold. If you leave this arrangement to the discretion of the company, a court may infer that you agreed to be bound by the company's decision. In one recent case, a salesman was denied commissions even though the company shipped $30,000 worth of off-price goods into his territory.

Cautious salesmen have their contracts specifically refer to the payment of commissions for off-price goods. You should leave nothing to the company's discretion. Do not allow the company to decide when the discount price is sufficiently close to the actual selling price to warrant the payment of commissions.

For protection, salesmen should include the following type of provision in their contract:

> The Salesman shall receive a commission rate of 8 percent. In the event that the Company reduces its price on its regular goods, the Salesman shall nonetheless be entitled to receive commissions on their sales. Commissions shall be determined by the following formula: Goods sold by either party at 75 percent of their original selling price shall result in a commission rate of 75 percent of 8 percent, or 6 percent; goods sold by either party at 50 percent of their original selling price shall result in a commission rate of 50 percent of 8 percent, or 4 percent; goods sold by either party at 25 percent or less of their original selling price shall result in a commission rate of 25 percent of 8 percent, or 2 percent.

If this provision is unacceptable, the alternative clause may be agreeable to the company:

Whereupon reduction of price on regular goods or off-price goods is given to the purchaser, the Salesman and Company must mutually agree upon a reduction of a commission rate. This rate must be negotiated in good faith by both parties. In no event shall the Salesman receive a commission rate for such goods that is lower than 4 percent.

Both provisions will protect your right to commissions for off-price goods.

D. VOLUNTARY RESIGNATIONS: WHEN DO COMMISSIONS CEASE?

The law treats salesmen harshly when they voluntarily leave their jobs in the middle of a selling season or calendar quarter. This is so even if they give proper notice. Courts have consistently ruled that salesmen are not entitled to receive commissions on sales for orders shipped *after* resignation. The law penalizes salesmen by strictly enforcing the terms of their contract and only awarding compensation for commissions actually earned up to the date of resignation.

Salesmen have not been able to recover commissions on sales the company made following resignation even though they were responsible for procuring the listing of the company's products in prestigious catalogs. Furthermore, salesmen are usually *not* entitled to commissions on shipments made after their contracts have terminated which stem from open-end orders procured by them prior to resignation.

This harsh treatment also applies to salesmen who are responsible for servicing as well as selling company products. If goods have been shipped before resignation and a salesman has a duty to service those orders in the future, he may lose the right to such commissions, particularly if that is the custom in his industry.

For protection, salesmen can include a provision in their contract similar in effect to the following:

> *If the Salesman shall leave the employ of the Company before the expiration of the agreed-upon term (one year), he shall receive commissions on all orders accepted by the Company, which upon such resignation date have been either unaccepted or accepted but unshipped, but are eventually accepted and shipped by the Company before the natural expiration of such agreed-upon term.*

This will allow you to receive commissions for orders that are accepted by the company after your resignation.

If you are responsible for servicing your company's products, the following clause will protect your interests:

> *In the event of termination of this contract the Salesman shall receive commission on all accepted sales prior to the termination date. No condition or obligation on the part of the Salesman shall preclude his right to obtain commission on such sales.*

1. Secured Accounts for Key Account Salesmen

Some salesmen are specifically hired for the purpose of introducing new accounts to the company. Other company representatives then sell the product. In the past, courts have awarded commissions to such key account salesmen. To recover, a salesman must be able to prove that his efforts were indispensable in cementing a business relationship between his company and the subsequent buyer, and he must show that his efforts *alone* landed the account due to his unique personality, experience, contacts, and forceful selling habits.

Salesmen who have been hired mainly to introduce new accounts to their company should have their contracts clearly indicate this arrangement. If possible, such contracts should also include a clause stating that the salesman will be able to obtain commissions for sales made by other employees of the company even after the salesman resigns or his contract is terminated.

Helpful Hints

If you are the primary cause in obtaining a lucrative account and then other company representatives are about to take over and do the actual selling, obtain *written* assurances that you will receive subsequent commissions stemming from this account. It would be better to include this in your contract before you begin working.

2. Lump Sum Payments

Salesmen should *never* agree to solicit orders throughout the year and receive commissions in one lump sum at the end of the contract term. In the past, courts have construed this arrangement to mean that the parties agreed that the company would pay commissions only after the salesman rendered services for the *entire* period.

For example, Stacey is a sales representative who resigned from her job three months before the time her contract specified commissions would be paid. Because of this arrangement, she forfeited all commissions on sales made up to the resignation date.

Learn from Stacey's mistake. Always specify that commissions are to be paid biweekly or monthly, and never in one lump sum at the natural expiration of the employment agreement.

E. REORDERS

Even though the law treats salespeople unfavorably when they resign from their jobs, courts sometimes award commissions for merchandise reorders. Reorders are repeats of merchandise previously purchased by the customer. Salesmen often have difficulty proving that reorders were involved (for example, the exact style or model number) and shipped. To avoid such problems, salesmen should include a provision in their contract similar to the following:

> Upon termination, for the additional period of one year, the Salesman shall receive full commission on all reorders shipped by the Company, even though such

shipments are made after resignation or termination of the Salesman's services. The Salesman shall have the right to inspect the Company's books and records for this purpose.

This clause will obligate the company to pay you commissions for reorders regardless of arrangements with other salesmen. However, you will not be able to obtain commissions on reorders if you wrongfully breach your contract.

Helpful Hints

If you have this arrangement, call certain accounts periodically to determine whether they placed reorders. Then check your records and commission statements to see if you received proper credit.

F. IF YOU ARE TERMINATED

All salesmen should insist upon the right to receive written notice in advance of termination, since the benefits are considerable. After notice is given, you will receive commissions for orders that have been accepted and shipped between the notice and termination date. However, if you assent to the immediate termination, you may only recover commissions earned up to the date when notice was given. One salesman made this mistake and he was denied extra commissions.

G. WRONGFUL TERMINATION AND COMMISSIONS

If a salesman is discharged in bad faith, courts frequently rule that a company should not be able to profit by its wrongful acts. The effect of this principle can be illustrated by the following example. Suppose your contract states that you are to receive commissions for all sales in your territory. If you are terminated with proper notice shortly before bids are to be opened on a government contract within your territory, you may be entitled to commissions on future sales once the bid is successful, especially if your contract was terminated in bad faith and the company fired you to avoid paying commissions. Even if you played no part in helping to obtain the contract, courts may not permit the company to use its right of termination to defeat your claims for compensation.

However, proving bad faith is very difficult and commissions are rarely awarded, since salesmen have a hard time demonstrating that they were terminated for "bad faith" reasons. On the other hand, if you have been constantly producing increased sales and have established significant reorder potential, then being fired may be sufficient to infer bad faith on the part of the company.

H. ADDITIONAL COMMISSION PROBLEMS

1. The Company Sells Your Division While You Are Working

Assume that Robin, an independent selling agent, has been working three years for a company. Her contract stated that commissions would be earned by accepted orders and that commissions would be payable for goods sold up to six months after termination. All orders were subject to the company's final written acceptance, and the company reserved an absolute right to refuse acceptance of orders.

During her employment term the company sells its assets to another company, resulting in an elimination of Robin's division. She stops soliciting orders several weeks after receiving written notice, and the company does not accept any of her most recent orders. Robin receives an accurate commission statement and commission check.

Although a favorable ruling for salesmen in this situation is not always certain, these were the very facts of a recent case in which a salesman sued his company. He argued that he was entitled to receive commissions on all orders that would have been placed within six months from the termination date had the company not sold its business. He *was successful.* The court stated that the company had violated its agreement with the salesman, since it had become impossible to receive the salesman's services in a manner contemplated by the contract. Even though the company had a right to sell its business and reject the salesman's orders, the court stated that the company could not deprive the salesman of future commissions.

2. The Commission Rate Is Altered

Let us examine another common situation. Herb is a sales representative who is working for a company at an 8 percent commission rate. One day he is told that he will receive a 6 percent rate for all new orders that he solicits in the future. His contract does not contain any provision allowing the company to change the commission rate. What should Herb do?

In this situation Herb may have no choice but to continue working. If he is in the middle of a selling season, he has invested time and money in his product line. However, there are ways in which he can protect himself. Herb can take the following steps.

A letter should be sent to the company. It should state, as diplomatically as possible, that the salesman intends to continue working under the terms of the original contract. However, he must be subtle. If he has an employment at will contract, this may cause the company to fire him. The documentation of this protest will ensure that his subsequent conduct will not be viewed as an acceptance of the new commission rate, and the salesman in this fashion preserves his rights to the higher commission even though he continues to work and cash the checks paying the lower rate. Herb remembered that a contract could only be modified by express agreement of *both* parties (see Section 9). In addition, after the selling season, Herb should insist again that he receive the difference that was withheld.

Helpful Hints

To protect yourself from company exploitation, the following provision may be included in your contract:

The Company agrees to pay the Salesman as compensation for his services a commission rate of 8 percent. This commission rate shall exist for the entire duration of the agreement, and can only be modified upon the express written consent of both the Company and the Salesman.

3. Residual Commissions

Lawyers have begun arguing that a salesman is entitled to recover a percentage of residual sales from accounts within his territory that he originally introduced to the company and that continue to purchase company products after the salesman no longer works for the company. In one recent case a salesman was awarded money for residual sales. In the expectation that he would be offered a "piece of the business," he performed services for a newly formed company by designing a product and locating purchasers. When he was offered a smaller percentage of the stock than he would have liked, he did not accept this compensation. He sued the company to recover residual commissions for the reasonable value of his services. The court ruled that under an unjust enrichment theory (see Section 12), the salesman was entitled to a commission rate of 5 percent of all sales from the design for a period of two years. This amounted to a substantial amount of money.

Salesmen should attempt to have their companies grant commissions on residual sales whenever possible. If this arrangement is agreed upon, you should have it stated *in writing.* You may wish to include the following provision in your contract:

> *The Company agrees to pay the Salesman residual commissions of 2 percent on all sales of goods purchased by account X for a period of twelve months after the date of the Salesman's resignation or termination.*

If you obtain a residual commission provision, consult with an attorney to ensure that it is properly drafted.

4. The Salesman as Guarantor

Some salesmen guarantee the accounts they do business with. This guarantee may take the form of the following:

*I (Salesman) personally guarantee that all monies due
from store X will be paid to the Company. If the above
account has any default payments due Company, I
hereby authorize the Company to deduct the above
monies from my commission.*

Signed and Dated
(Salesman)

Written guarantees such as these are enforceable, especially if signed and witnessed. No particular form of expression is needed to make the guarantee valid, and the word "guarantee" does not have to appear on the face of the document.

Salesmen should avoid signing guarantees whenever possible, since they may find themselves involved in bitter disputes with their companies over collection proceedings. Unless the guarantee expressly states otherwise, salesmen may be personally liable for nonpayment arising from *any* reason. Thus, for example, if the company ships damaged goods that the account refuses to pay for and the company does not acknowledge that it shipped defective merchandise, the salesmen would have to reimburse the company as a result of the account's failure to pay.

If you are about to sign a guarantee, read the following helpful hints before doing so.

Helpful Hints

1. Assure your employer that the account will pay its bills on time. Avoid putting this in writing since guarantees must be in writing in some states to be legally enforceable.

2. When the company asks you to sign a written guarantee, try to compromise by agreeing that you will not be paid for commissions on defaulting or late paying accounts until the company has been paid in full, or that commissions paid on these accounts may be repaid to the company by the salesman.

3. If your company insists on a written guarantee, include the following provision:

The Company agrees that in return for this guarantee, it will exercise due and reasonable diligence in collecting the monies from said account.

This clause prevents the company from withholding your commissions if they fail to act.

Note also that you do not have to pay for costs arising from the lawsuit unless the guarantee specifically says so.

4. Include conditions that will avoid the imposition of personal liability. For example:

The Salesman is not responsible and will not be required to assume personal liability for nonpayment caused by the negligence of the Company. Examples of negligence include misbranded or damaged goods sent by the Company which the account refuses to pay for.

5. Specify the maximum amount of money for which you will be personally liable. State that you will not be liable for the full price of goods or merchandise that the company later sells at a lower price.

6. Specify how long the guarantee is to last. Make sure that it does not continue indefinitely and has an express cutoff date. For example:

This guarantee will exist only for sales to account X for the months of April and May 1981.

7. Insist on a clause that states that the company must send you written notice before withholding your commissions.

8. Try to obtain written permission granting you the option to sue the customer on your own behalf.

9. Attempt to include a clause that gives you the right to revoke the guarantee upon written notice.

10. If the account has failed to pay, call them daily and insist that they promptly pay your company for the goods that they purchased. This should be done first since they may decide to pay before being subjected to litigation and you may not wish to lose them as an account.

11. Be certain that the company is obligated to inform you that the account has not paid within the terms specified

(that is, net thirty days) so that you can immediately make inquiries.

12. Be certain that the company does not have the right to give the account any extended terms or that if this occurs you are no longer obligated under the guarantee.

13. Try to ship C.O.D. only to these accounts.

I. COMPANY SUITS TO RECOVER EXCESS ADVANCES

Salesmen and other employees are often advanced money designated as "draw" to be applied against and reimbursed by future commissions. These are designated in employment agreements as "draw against commission" or "advances against commission." The "draw against commission" is an integral part of the working relationship between the salesman and his company, since the salesman often spends his time and effort to secure orders for the company and does not receive commissions on those orders for several months.

This section will discuss the personal liability of salesmen who, after leaving their company, have received advances that exceed their commissions.

1. The General Rule of Personal Liability

When an oral agreement or written contract of employment states that advances will be deducted from commissions to be earned in the future, the salesman is *not* personally liable to pay any excess from his own pocket unless he promised to do so. The reason for this rule is that courts generally consider advances to be *additional salary* unless language in the agreement and the conduct of both parties expressly indicates that such advances were merely intended to be a loan.

The law considers the company to be in a superior bargaining position. This makes the company responsible to clearly indicate its right of repayment. Past cases reveal that most company lawsuits to recover excess advances are unsuccessful, since ambiguous language in a contract is almost always applied against the company who chose the language and drafted the document.

Even if a salesman leaves the company before his employment term has expired, this will not necessarily make him liable to return the excess. However, if he breached his agreement, courts will not permit him to profit from his wrongful acts. Wrongdoing occurs when the salesman constructively abandons his job by primarily selling sidelines, or acts unfaithfully by leaving early to form a rival company.

2. Factors Indicating an Express Agreement to Repay

Words in an agreement suggestive of indebtedness, such as "loan," "debt," "charge," or "obligation," are usually not sufficient alone to make the salesman liable. A court will then examine the conduct of both parties very closely. The following examples were taken from actual cases where salesmen were found to be personally liable. You may wish to protect yourself by:

1. Avoid signing any written contract which states that advances are not considered part payment of salary but rather personal indebtedness to be applied against and reimbursed by commissions earned in the future;

2. Avoid signing or endorsing checks containing the word "loan" on the face of the check;

3. Avoid signing and returning any letters to the company which state that such advances are loans;

4. Avoid signing any indemnification, loan agreement, financing statement, or promissory note to the same effect;

5. Avoid signing receipts for advances that indicate a promise to repay; and

6. Avoid acknowledging to anyone that you *intend to repay any excess advances.*

Salesmen often make the mistake of promising to repay excess advances. Such a promise may make them liable for repayment. Always object in writing if you receive statements that indicate that you owe the company money because of commission deficits. This will document your protest in the event that litigation eventually follows.

Perhaps the best way to protect yourself from personal

liability is to include a provision in your contract similar to the following:

> *The Company shall advance the Salesman $X per week which is to be used by the Salesman to cover his travel and incidental expenses, and is to be charged against him as a drawing account and deducted from any amounts due Salesman as commissions. Any excess of said drawing account over and above the amount of commissions due at the end of this agreement or any renewal thereof shall not be a personal charge against the Salesman and there shall be no liability upon the Salesman to refund any excess of drawing account over commissions.*

3. Oral Contracts and Their Effect

Oral employment contracts make it quite difficult for companies to prove that salesmen expressly promised to re-pay excess advances. If the salesman does not acknowledge a duty to repay, this issue will generally be resolved in his favor.

4. New Contracts and Their Effect

If you enter into a new agreement and you orally prom-ise to repay money overdrawn under a previous agreement, you probably will not be responsible for repayment if the new contract does not state this oral promise. In addition, if your old contract is extended and you sign a document acknowl-edging that you owe money to the company, some courts state that you will not be liable unless your promise to repay was given in exchange for additional and valuable consideration.

J. SALESMEN'S SUITS TO RECOVER ADVANCES FOR THE ENTIRE TERM

Companies often promise to advance money for the entire term of the contract. However, these payments may be stopped because of changes in policy after the company deter-mines that the advances will not be offset by earned commissions. Some salesmen have sued to recover these remaining advances. They have encountered difficulties, since it is necessary to prove that such advances were *guaranteed.*

In such suits, courts look at the specific contract provisions and decide whether these guarantee the salesman a minimum amount of money or whether the compensation is to be derived solely from earned commissions. If there is an oral agreement, a company may be obligated to pay money (regardless of the earning of commissions) if they promised to advance the salesman a specified amount periodically. New York decisions have been especially sympathetic to salesmen on this issue.

Helpful Hints

To increase your chances of success in this type of lawsuit, avoid signing an agreement that gives the company the right to cancel advances without notice.

SECTION 5
TERRITORIAL RIGHTS

A territory is the area that a salesman canvasses in order to obtain orders and service his accounts. Problems pertaining to territorial rights arise when the terms of the salesman's working arrangement are ambiguous or his territory is not properly defined. Your contract should specify whether or not you are the exclusive selling agent and what area your territory comprises. For example, it should state the following:

> *The Company agrees to pay the Salesman as compensation for his services a commission of 8 percent on the net amount of sales made, shipped, and/or distributed into the Salesman's territory, consisting of the following states, in which the Salesman shall have exclusive territorial rights: New Jersey, Pennsylvania, Delaware, Maryland, and Washington, D.C.*

A. EXCLUSIVE SELLING AGENT

If you are the only sales representative to sell company goods in a particular territory, insist that the term "exclusive selling agent" appear in your contract. Avoid using other terms that are unclear and ambiguous. For example, if the term "nonexclusive selling agent" appears in your contract and you are involved in a lawsuit, it would be the court's function to determine what that term really meant. You would then have the difficult burden of proving that it was the established custom in your industry that no representative would work an area unless he had an exclusive right to sell the product. Thus, if applicable, include the magic words "exclusive selling agent" to avoid problems for all parties concerned.

B. YOUR COMMISSIONS

If you receive commissions on sales made by others in your territory, make sure that your contract specifies this. Your contract should clearly state whether you will receive commissions only for orders that you personally sell, or whether you will receive commissions on orders for goods shipped into your territory that were sold by other company representatives. The following clause illustrates this:

> The Company agrees to give the Salesman credit for all sales made in Salesman's territory, whether the orders for such sales are sent by the Salesman, or received by the Company through the mail, or taken at the Company's place of business by other Salesmen without the assistance or presence of the Salesman.

If you have an exclusive territory and you permit other salesmen to sell related products in your territory, have your contract state that you will receive an additional percentage "override" for these sales.

When a company appoints a salesman as its exclusive sales representative in a specified territory, this arrangement does not violate federal laws relating to restraint of trade. The

Federal Trade Commission, which enforces the Clayton Act, has stated that companies who engage in interstate commerce may sell their product exclusively through one salesman in a given territory and the company's refusal to have others sell in such territory is not unlawful. Thus, you and your company are protected from other salesmen if they claim that your exclusive territorial rights arrangement is unfair.

C. YOUR TERRITORY

Most salesman are limited to receiving commissions for orders that are placed in their territory. However, there are a number of occasions when a salesman's efforts result in orders being received from customers outside of the salesman's territory. Here is a common situation: Salesman A solicits an account in Massachusetts, his exclusive territory. The account may act as a buying office for its chain stores and then ship the goods to stores located in Rhode Island and Vermont. These accounts are not located in Salesman A's territory, and each pays for the goods separately. Salesman A does not receive commissions for the orders in Rhode Island and Vermont, since the stores are not within his territory. Instead, the company credits the commissions to Salesman B because of his exclusive territorial rights arrangement in the states of Rhode Island and Vermont. To avoid this, Salesman A should specify the following in writing:

> In the event that the Salesman obtains orders from an account in his territory and the Company ships goods to this account, the Salesman shall receive full credit for such sales, regardless if the goods are then distributed into another territory and/or paid for by an account in another territory.

D. HOUSE ACCOUNTS

House accounts are those customers and retail stores that the company considers off limits and nonsolicitable by its salesmen. Salesmen are unable to receive commissions from these accounts even if they have exclusive territorial rights. However, courts have ruled that salesmen are entitled to sell to and receive commissions from all accounts within their territory unless their contracts *specifically designate* certain accounts as house accounts.

In one recent case a salesman received a contract in the form of a letter. It confirmed that he would represent a particular line and obtain a commission rate of 6 percent for all net sales to accounts within his designated territory. Several weeks later he and the company argued about the status of a particularly large account after the company claimed that it was a house account. The salesman resigned and sued. The court ruled that since the account had not been mentioned in the contract as a house account, the words *"for all net sales"* were unambiguous. Thus, the court stated that the company's failure to pay for this account constituted a breach of the salesman's contract and awarded him commissions.

E. SELLING IN OTHER TERRITORIES

If you would like to sell to other accounts located outside of your designated territory and the company does not object, you may include the following type of provision in your contract:

> *Out of territory accounts sold by the Salesman at trade shows, etc., will be given full credit and full commission payment.*

Salesmen are often asked by the company to sell in another territory. If you are requested to do this, make sure that you obtain company permission and have the company specify in writing the commission rate that you will be paid for these sales. In addition, if another salesman already sells in that territory, obtain written acknowledgment giving you permission to sell in his territory.

SECTION 6
PROPER ACCOUNTING

Proper accounting is vital for any salesman who works on a commission basis. Most salesmen rely on the honesty and integrity of their companies as to the accuracy of the figures that are presented to them. In most instances companies do give a proper accounting. However, many employers use questionable methods of record keeping. Salesmen have been victimized tens of thousands of dollars by employers who have failed to record sales properly and render credit for all shipped orders.

These are just a few of the abuses either intentionally or unintentionally practiced upon salesmen. Since to err is human, salesmen should have a means of checking their employers' figures because even the most honorable companies make mistakes.

All too often a salesman will simply quit his job when he learns that he is being cheated out of commissions. He may feel that the amount of money at issue is too small to warrant the trouble and expense of instituting legal action. Salesmen with this attitude deserve to get "ripped off." Remember that you can always sue your company quickly and inexpensively by filing a complaint in Small Claims Court (see Section 16). Furthermore, the amount that you know has been withheld might be just the tip of the iceberg. If your company has not accounted for some of the money that is owed, there may be much more that belongs to you. This section will explain how to discover what is owed and how you can protect yourself from your employer's "mistakes."

A. PROPER ACCOUNTING PROVISIONS

The best way to avoid the problems of improper accounting is to take preventative measures that ensure that your commission statements will be accurate. This can be done by having a clause in your contract that states the following:

> *The Company agrees to furnish the Salesman with a copy of all invoices and orders concerning any goods shipped into the Salesman's territory or sold to customers therein, and to furnish the Salesman with a statement on the fifteenth (15) of each month covering the amount of sales for the previous month and the amount of commissions due the Salesman. The Company will keep an accurate set of records with regard to all commissions and further agrees that the Salesman may appoint a certified public accountant who shall, upon the Salesman's written request, have access to all of the Company's books and records relating to such commissions during regular business hours, for the purpose of verifying commission statements thereunder.*

This provision allows you to check your figures with those of your company. It is strongly suggested that such a clause appear in your contract. Insist upon it.

Many employers impose a duty on their salesmen to keep records and accounts that the company then relies upon. The following provision is an example:

> *All books, accounts, or other documents relating to the business of the Company are the property of the Company whether paid for by it or not, and they shall be subject at all times to inspection by a duly authorized representative of the Company and shall be delivered to the Company by the Sales Representative on the termination of this agreement.*

If you have such a clause in your contract, maintain a second set of records for yourself. When you leave your job, you will then have a means of checking if your company fulfilled all of its payment obligations.

B. LEGAL ACTION FOR PROPER ACCOUNTING

If you have evidence that the company owes you money, you may want to compel your company to furnish the records so that either you or your accountant can review them. This can be done whether or not there is a proper accounting provision in your contract. You would then sue your company for damages based upon the amount of money that was owed to you.

Companies have a legal obligation to keep records of all accounts, particularly if their salesmen receive commissions. This duty is most apparent after the salesman resigns or has been terminated, since it is virtually impossible to obtain information on sales figures for goods that were shipped and paid for after the salesman left the company's employ.

If your employer will not voluntarily turn over this information to you, it may be necessary to compel him to do so by means of discovery procedures. Discovery procedures play an important role in virtually every lawsuit, and both parties use them in order to obtain information before the case is brought to trial.

It first must be established to the court's satisfaction that money is due and owing before you are entitled to examine the records of your company. You cannot ransack your employer's books and records in the hope that something helpful will turn up. However, if you can show that the company's documents and records will help your case, discovery will usually be allowed by the court.

C. REVIEWING YOUR RECORDS

1. Computer Errors

The fact that you get a computer printout commission statement does *not* mean that you are obtaining 100 percent accurate accounting. Duplicate invoices are often photocopied in error. In addition, some companies give each of their salesmen a different computer number. If these numbers are fed into the computer incorrectly, other salesmen will receive credit for your sales. You should also be particularly careful if your invoices are delayed and the company informs you that you will receive supplementary sheets at a later date. Many salesmen forget to tally these sheets and lose valuable commissions.

2. Your Personal Records

In order to prove that you have a justifiable reason to view your company's books during pretrial discovery, you may be asked to provide information that reveals what you are looking for. Usually these requests must be supported by written documentation. For example, you may have to make specific references to accounts and you may be required to furnish the dates of the sale in addition to the products that were sold. Thus, save *all* of your records.

3. Your Commission Statement

Check your commission statements carefully when you receive them. These contain the commission rate you received on earlier orders, the account, and the date of shipment to that customer. You should call certain key accounts periodically to discover what was shipped to them. Then, compare this with the orders, shipping lists, and invoices you received from the company and check all of this against your commission statement. Although this will require additional effort, you will benefit both economically and professionally. Even if no errors are discovered, you will have reviewed the current needs and purchases of your customers.

Helpful Hints

When reviewing your commission statements, do not forget to question all house accounts, accounts that are sold at a reduced rate, and the credits and shipping charges that have been applied against your commissions.

3

COMPETING WITH YOUR COMPANY

SECTION 7
DUTIES OF THE SALESMAN

A. DUTIES WHILE WORKING FOR THE COMPANY

Courts strictly impose a duty of loyalty upon salesmen. This duty exists throughout the salesman's employment with his company and is also present when the salesman changes jobs and joins a new company.

1. Duty Not to Exceed Authority

A salesman's authority is usually defined by the terms of his employment contract with the company. If a salesman exceeds this authority, he is responsible for the consequences of his unauthorized acts. For instance, Jonathan, a manufacturer's representative, quoted a price for machine parts that was below the list price in order to obtain a large order. He hoped that he could convince his employer to agree to the reduced price. His hopes did not materialize. Jonathan had to pay the difference between the list price and the price he quoted. Thus, salesmen should *never* promise discounts that are lower than the quoted company rate unless they have specific authorization to do so.

2. Duty Not to Work for a Competitor

A salesman can inform his customers that he intends to leave his job and work for a competitor. However, a salesman cannot work for a competitor while he is still employed by his present company. In one recent case a salesman told customers that he intended to leave his company to work for a competitor. He then distributed the competitor's catalogs to these customers. He was terminated by his former company and had to pay a considerable amount of money in damages for his disloyal actions.

Many companies will not allow a salesman to sell noncompeting goods. The following clause in a contract is an example of such an arrangement:

> *The Sales Representative agrees to devote his entire time, skill, labor, and attention to this Company during the term of his employment.*

If this type of clause appears in your contract, you *cannot* sell another line or product. If you do, you can be sued for damages, and in the event of a lawsuit you may have to pay the company a significant portion of the money that you earned from these sales.

If you want to sell a noncompeting sideline for another company, the following clause should be included in your contract:

> *The Salesman may carry additional lines provided that no additional lines are conflicting.*

Salesmen should *never* sell competing lines unless their company is aware of this and both the salesman and the company sign an agreement acknowledging that the company does not object to this arrangement.

3. Duty Not to Make Secret Profits

A salesman cannot make deals with customers in which he promises to perform favors in return for secret kickbacks involving money or vacations. If you engage in such conduct without the company's knowledge and consent, the company can terminate your employment and sue you for damages.

B. DUTIES AFTER LEAVING THE COMPANY

After leaving the company, many salesmen either work for a competitor or compete directly against their former companies. Salesmen are free to do this as long as a restrictive covenant is not contained in their contract (see Section 8). However, a salesman can be sued for damages if he reveals the trade secrets or confidential information of his former company.

1. Trade Secrets

A trade secret is a secret process or formula known only by a few people. If you learn trade secrets while working for a company, you cannot reveal them once you leave your job. For instance, one salesman obtained knowledge in confidence about the manufacturing process of certain cosmetics. The court prohibited him from using this process to compete against his former employer.

2. Confidential Information

The most frequently disputed issue with respect to confidential information concerns customer lists. Generally, a salesman *can* use a customer list if such information was readily accessible to all persons in the industry. If the names of customers can be obtained from a telephone book, the list is not confidential. In addition, the names and addresses of route customers are generally not confidential. Thus, when Kerri, a former driver-saleswoman for a linen supply company, went to work for a competitor, she was allowed to solicit her old customers.

However, there are certain instances when a salesman will *not* be allowed to use customer lists. They cannot be used:

a. If the salesman secretly copies the list and his customers were not publicly listed;

b. If the employer spent considerable time, effort, and money in compiling the list; and

c. If the employer kept the list under lock and key or generally took great care to protect its secrecy.

If a salesman becomes friendly with customers in the course of his previous employment, he will generally be allowed to call on them for his new employer. However, a salesman is prohibited from using his knowledge of the customer's buying habits, requirements, or other information when soliciting his former employer's customers. If the salesman knows that a particular customer will be in short supply of a product, he cannot solicit that customer while working for a competitor.

3. Consequences for Revealing Trade Secrets and Confidential Information

If a salesman reveals trade secrets or confidential information, a court may issue an injunction (order) prohibiting him from using this information and prohibiting him from calling upon former customers. The injunction usually lasts for a period of time, for example, one year. In addition, the salesman would probably be sued for damages. This could amount to thousands of dollars.

SECTION 8
RESTRICTIVE COVENANTS IN EMPLOYMENT CONTRACTS

A. WHAT IS A RESTRICTIVE COVENANT?

Restrictive covenants are provisions in contracts that do not allow the salesman to directly compete or work for a competitor after leaving his old company. In essence, they "box" salesmen in and are included in contracts because the company does not wish to lose its customers. Such covenants may:

1. Restrict the salesman from working for a competitor of his former company;

2. Restrict the salesman from starting his own business that competes with his former company;

3. Restrict the territory in which the salesman can seek reemployment in a similar line of work; and

4. Contain a time period that provides how long these restrictions can last.

The following is an example of a restrictive covenant:

The Sales Representative shall not, for a period of one year after he ceases to be a Sales Representative of this Company, solicit, sell, or in any way assist in the soliciting or selling of products similar to those he sold for the Company in the territory he was assigned while working under the terms of this contract.

In the absence of a restrictive covenant the law does not prevent a salesman from competing with his former company.

B. RESTRAINTS ON TERRITORY AND TIME

If you have a restrictive covenant in your employment contract, you may be prevented from working in a territory ranging from a city, county, or even the entire United States. There are no formulas that define what territory may be excluded. However, a number of state courts have refused to enforce restrictive covenants if the area of the restriction was beyond the salesman's former sales territory.

Many courts allow these covenants to remain in effect for a year or two, and some have been enforced up to ten years depending upon the degree of skill and training of the particular salesman. In determining how long a restriction is reasonable, courts often consider how long it will take the former company to train a replacement in addition to deciding how long it will take for the salesman's "hold" over his former customers to diminish.

C. UNENFORCEABLE RESTRICTIVE COVENANTS

If you sign a restrictive covenant, you may not be bound by its terms. Restrictive covenants are not enforced by courts in certain instances. You will learn what these areas are in the following section.

1. Independent Selling Agents

In a number of states, if you are an independent selling agent, it is illegal for a company to restrain you from working for a competitor. Thus, if a restrictive covenant were in your contract, it could not be enforced against you. However, if you are not considered to be an independent selling agent, but rather an employee (see Section 3), the restriction is valid and the company can sue you to have the covenant enforced.

2. Unreasonable Terms in the Restrictive Covenant

Many employment contracts contain restrictive covenants that are unreasonable because they are either for too long a period of time or else they unfairly restrict a salesman's ability to work in a geographical territory.

If the covenant is found to be unreasonable, courts either declare the entire clause to be void and refuse to enforce it, or else decide that the clause is overbroad, and either shorten the time period or narrow the geographical area to which the covenant will be applied. For example, Richard signed a contract which contained a restrictive covenant in order to be hired by a prestigious company. The covenant stated that when he left the company he could not work for any competitor in the states of New York and Connecticut for three years. Two years later, Richard terminated his contract and began to work for a competitor. His former company sued. The court found the covenant to be unreasonable and modified it, preventing Richard from working only in the state of New York for one year.

There is no precise definition that states what makes a restrictive covenant reasonable. The relevant considerations that a court looks at when deciding to enforce a covenant are:

a. The hardship to the salesman if it is enforced;

b. Whether any special skills and training were involved;

c. Whether the salesman had access to trade secrets;

d. Whether the salesman had access to confidential information such as customer lists, specific business methods, established routes, and credit information; and

e. The bargaining power of the parties.

3. Subsequent Adoption of a Restrictive Covenant

If your company requires you to sign a restrictive covenant after you begin working, some state courts will not enforce it unless the company gives you a corresponding benefit. This may include an increase in salary, commission, or a change in job status. If you do not receive additional compensation, the covenant may not be enforceable. However, other states do not require you to receive extra benefits in order for the covenant to be enforceable. Thus, consult with an attorney if you are about to sign a covenant not to compete with your company.

4. Salesmen Who Lack Special Skills or Knowledge of Trade Secrets

If the salesman's services are not special, unique, or extraordinary, some states will not enforce a restrictive covenant. For example, many cases have held that restrictive covenants are *not* enforceable with respect to house-to-house salesmen because no special skills were involved in the sale of the items they solicited.

Likewise, restrictive covenants may not be enforceable if trade secrets are not involved. Salesmen with knowledge of customer lists that can be obtained from sources of public access, such as telephone books, cannot be restrained from working for another company.

5. Company Breach of Contract

You may not be bound by the terms of a restrictive covenant if the company breaches your contract (see Chapter 5).

If it fails to pay you commissions, you generally have the right to quit your job and work for a competitor immediately. However, contact an attorney before embarking upon this course of action.

D. CONSEQUENCES OF VIOLATING THE RESTRICTIVE COVENANT

Despite the fact that the restrictive covenant in the employment contract prohibits the salesman from working for a competitor prior to the time specified in the contract, many salesmen do secure positions with competitors. If this occurs, the salesman will have breached his contract and the company can sue for damages or seek injunctive relief.

Most courts will grant injunctive relief rather than damages. Injunctive relief results when the court issues an order (injunction) that prohibits the salesman from working for the company's competitor. If you fail to comply with this court order, you will be held in contempt of court.

However, if the salesman believes he is correct, his attorney may request permission of the court to post bond for the damages a company might be awarded so that the salesman can continue to sell for the competitor.

Helpful Hints

If you signed a contract that contained a restrictive covenant and you no longer work for the company, have the company sign a *waiver* or release (for an example of a waiver, see Chapter 5) if the covenant is still enforceable and you want to work for a competing company. Once the company signs a waiver, it will no longer have a legal claim against you. However, you may have to pay the company money in order to obtain this. Consult with an attorney to ensure that the waiver adequately protects your interests.

The best method of protection is simply the following: Never sign a contract that contains a restrictive covenant if you can help it!

CHANGING YOUR CONTRACTUAL RELATIONSHIP

SECTION 9
MODIFICATION OF THE CONTRACT

A. WHAT IS A MODIFICATION?

A modification of a contract occurs when terms of your agreement are either added, changed, or removed. These changes will be viewed as modifications as long as the general purpose and effect of the original contract remains the same. For instance, if a salesman's territory is altered yet his rate of commission, employment term, and other duties of his job remain unchanged, his agreement to sell in a new territory is a modification of the old contract. If the contract has been modified, the new terms replace the old terms and the parts of the contract that were not modified remain unaffected by these changes.

A salesman or his company can modify their contract as long as they both consent to all changes. Thus, if a company seeks to reduce the salesman's rate of commission and the salesman objects, the company cannot alter the salesman's commission rate.

An agreement by the parties to modify the contract does not have to be in writing. In certain situations courts have found that the salesman and his company consented to a modification of the contract as a result of changes in their working relationship. This can be illustrated by the following example. If the company decides to lower your commission rate and you do not object, a court will probably find that you consented to the change by your actions even though you never agreed to the lower rate. You must actually refuse to accept all unfavorable modifications. However, if your employment contract is terminable at will, you may have little choice but to accept the proposed modification since an objection may result in your termination.

Modifications usually have to be supported by *consideration* to be enforceable. This means that if your contract is modified, you must receive, and your company must give up, something of value. However, courts do not impose this requirement of consideration for employment contracts as strictly as with other kinds of contracts. In an employment relationship, they treat the salesman's duties as ongoing, since he must continually seek new orders and service his customers. Thus, when a salesman's contract is modified, courts usually treat the original consideration he received when entering into the contract (i.e., his commissions and/or salary) as being sufficient to support modifications.

If you sign another agreement or addendum to the contract so that the two contracts differ on conditions regarding the same subject matter, the terms of the later agreement replace those of the earlier agreement. Thus, if your original contract was signed on January 1 and you sign a new agreement on May 1 that increases your commission rate, the May 1 agreement will be viewed as defining your rights to commissions.

B. CONTRACT PROVISIONS THAT LIMIT THE RIGHT TO MODIFY

A written contract may be modified by the salesman and his company even though the contract prohibits a modification in the manner that the parties have chosen. For instance, a contract may state that none of the terms contained within it may be modified. The following is an example of such a clause:

> *No change, addition, or erasure of any portion of this agreement shall be valid or binding upon either party.*

A contract may also provide that all modifications must be in writing. For example:

> *There may be no modifications of this agreement, except in writing, executed with the same formalities as required by this instrument.*

Despite these provisions, courts will allow the contract to be modified even if the change is not in writing. If the salesman and his company both orally agree to the modification, the written terms of the contract can be changed. In essence, provisions in a contract restricting modifications are unnecessary, since they generally do not have to be followed. However, all modifications should be in writing since written agreements are less subject to varying interpretations than oral agreements. In addition, some states will not enforce a modification unless it is in writing.

C. ORAL MODIFICATIONS OF WRITTEN CONTRACTS

As a general rule a written contract can be modified by an oral agreement reached after the salesman and his company have entered into their original contract. Salesmen should consult with an attorney to determine if the law in their state permits modification of written contracts by oral agreement. Assuming this is permitted, then, for example, even though a signed contract states that the salesman must pay for his samples, an oral modification may be agreed upon six months later whereupon the company agrees to furnish the samples for free and this new agreement will be binding. However, even if you are able to modify your contract orally, it is in your best interests to have. all changes made in writing.

D. ORAL MODIFICATIONS AND THE PAROL EVIDENCE RULE

Although written contracts can generally be modified by oral agreements, any oral modification must be made *after* the salesman and the company enter into their original contract. This is because of a legal principle referred to as the Parol Evidence Rule. In the event of a dispute, the Parol Evidence Rule will not permit the salesman or his company to introduce evidence regarding understandings they reached prior to entering into the written contract if the matters in dispute are specifically mentioned in the written agreement.

The law assumes that both parties have incorporated all of their intentions into the written contract. Thus, if the parties reach an oral understanding on January 2 that the commission rate for the salesman will be 6 percent, yet sign a contract fixing the commission rate at 5 percent on January 10, the salesman will be unable to introduce into evidence that the parties had agreed upon a rate of 6 percent.

However, a different result occurs if both sign a contract January 2 which states that the salesman will receive a 5 percent commission and the parties orally agree to raise the commission rate to 6 percent on January 10. Here the salesman *will* be able to introduce evidence showing that both he and the company had agreed upon a commission rate of 6 percent.

Despite the existence of the Parol Evidence Rule, there are situations where a salesman can introduce evidence of oral understandings reached with his company prior to the time their written contract was entered into. This will occur if:

1. The written contract is voidable for fraud, mistake, duress, undue influence, or illegality (see Section 10).

2. The matter in dispute is not mentioned or dealt with in the written contract. In this situation the law assumes that the parties did not intend the contract to nullify prior arrangements and they will be enforced. For example, if you and your company agree that the company would not deduct money for samples from commissions, and the contract does not men-

tion anything with respect to the treatment of samples, evidence could be introduced showing that the company promised to pay for them.

3. Information is needed to interpret ambiguous expressions, define the meaning of words, show evidence of established customs or usage in the trade, or add terms describing your obligations if these new terms are consistent with terms already in the contract. For instance, if your contract indicates that a certain territory has been assigned to you, the court may allow evidence regarding the custom in the industry to determine whether an exclusive territory was granted.

Helpful Hints

The following suggestions will be helpful should the issue of contract modifications arise:

1. If your company makes changes in your contract that you feel are intolerable, send the company a letter objecting to the changes. You should realize that this may result in the loss of your job, especially if you are employed at will.

2. If you receive a modification that is beneficial, make sure that the change is in writing. You do not have to write a new contract. Merely add an addendum to the old contract and have this dated and signed by yourself and the company. This can simply say:

> *The commission rate is hereby modified from 5 percent to 6 percent commencing on this date. All other provisions in this contract shall remain unchanged.*
>
> *(Signed and Dated)*

3. If your present contract has been orally modified, request a letter from your company verifying the changes that have been agreed upon.

4. Do *not* believe your company if it tells you that your present contract prevents either of you from modifying its terms.

5. Attempt to obtain the following "most favored party" modification clause:

Company agrees that if at any time during the term of this contract, the Company has in effect an agreement that gives or grants more favorable terms, conditions, or compensation to Sales Representatives similarly engaged in selling or promoting _____ (product or service) for the Company, and who receive the same class and type of _____ (product or service) as the Salesman, the Company shall notify the Salesman, in writing, with respect to the more favorable treatment, terms, conditions, or compensation. At his election, the Salesman may then request the Company to substitute this contract with a more favorable agreement, or, on an equivalent basis, amend this contract to give effect to such substitution.

This clause requires your company to grant you the option of modifying your contract when the company offers benefits to other salesmen that are more favorable than those you presently receive. This provision is particularly beneficial to salesmen who have been working for their companies for many years and consistently do a large volume of business.

SECTION 10
RESCISSION OF THE CONTRACT

A. WHAT IS RESCISSION?

Rescission occurs when a contract becomes "unmade." This relieves both the salesman and his company from further obligations. The contract is considered annulled, and both parties are restored to positions they occupied before the contract was entered into. The following is an example of a written agreement to rescind:

The employment agreement dated _____ has been rescinded. All rights, obligations, and duties of both parties stemming from this employment contract shall cease immediately and forever unless superseded by a new agreement between the parties. Both Salesman and Company agree that there is no longer a working relationship under the terms of their agreement dated _____.

Signed and Dated

A rescission of your contract does not necessarily have to be in writing. For example, it can arise in the following manner. You agree to work for a company and it sends you a sample line. After you work the line for a week you discover little interest in it, and another company has offered you a chance to sell its "hotter" line in the interim. Despite your written agreement, you tell your company that you "want out." It agrees to call the whole deal off after you return the line. Thus, the contract has been rescinded orally by mutual consent.

B. WHEN DOES RESCISSION OCCUR?

Contract rescissions can occur in one of the following ways:

1. By mutual consent between the company and the salesman;
2. By contract;
3. By either party on the ground of fraud, duress, or mistake; or
4. By a decree from the court.

1. Rescission by Mutual Consent

A salesman's contract can be rescinded anytime by mutual consent. The mutual consent may be expressed orally, in writing, or simply by conduct demonstrating such intention.

An oral understanding to rescind will be effective even if the employment contract is in writing. Thus, the words "Let's call the whole deal off" are sufficient to rescind your written contract.

If the contract is rescinded, the salesman and his company are still free to make a new contract. This new contract will now define the terms of the working relationship.

In order to determine if a valid rescission took place, courts look to the surrounding conduct and actions of the parties. They will decide whether an offer to rescind was accepted. This is important because if a company's offer to rescind is not accepted by the salesman, a rescission has not occurred and the salesman can still sue the company in court to enforce his contract.

Helpful Hints

1. If you decide to rescind your contract, whether it be a written contract or an oral agreement, have both parties sign a written rescission agreement.

2. Try to obtain all commissions and money owed to you before signing, or in any event, try to have the company agree to pay all earned commissions.

2. Rescission by Contract

A contract can provide for rescission automatically upon the happening of specified events. Once these events occur, the employment relationship has ended. The following provision is an illustration of this:

> *If the Company is purchased by another Company, and in the discretion of the Board of Directors a decision is reached to eliminate your division, then upon the giving of thirty days' written notice following such a decision, all rights, obligations, and duties of the parties under this contract shall cease.*

Clauses such as these are referred to as options to rescind. Most courts will enforce these options if the stated conditions are met. The company is then free from performing any remaining obligations.

Although these options are unfavorable, many salesmen are told that if they want to work they must sign contracts containing these types of clauses. However, the law does not allow companies to abandon their responsibilities with impunity. There is a catch. Options to rescind must be performed *exactly* as stated. Using the above provision as an example to illustrate this point, if a company failed to give you written notice of its decision to rescind your contract, such decision would not be binding. In addition, if the provision stated a specific time period for the company to rescind and that time had expired, the company could not rescind your contract after that date.

Provisions that fail to mention specified time limits must be performed within a reasonable time. A judge will decide what length of time is considered reasonable. Thus, if in the above situation the company was "bought out" and it decided to let you continue working for an additional six months, any decision to rescind your contract after that time would probably not be valid.

Helpful Hints

1. Avoid having options to rescind contained within your contract. If you are in a strong bargaining position, insist that this clause be removed from your contract.

2. If the company will not remove the clause, make sure that the option will not last forever. Insist that after a specified time the company cannot exercise the option.

3. Specify duties that the company must perform in order for the option to be effective. For example, require the company to send you written notice.

4. Avoid options that result in automatic termination upon the happening of stated conditions. An example of such an unfavorable clause follows:

> *If the Salesman is unable to secure three new accounts for the Company within the next sixty days, this contract shall terminate immediately and all rights, obligations, and duties on the part of the Company shall cease immediately.*

Require the company to take positive steps to rescind. This will increase the likelihood that the company will fail to act in the manner specified in the contract and may provide you with a remedy for breach of contract.

5. Consult an attorney if you feel that the option was unfair, exercised improperly, or if you were forced to agree to it.

3. Rescission by Fraud, Duress, or Mistake

A salesman can either rescind his contract or have a court do so if he can prove that his employment agreement was originally entered into as a result of either fraud, duress, or mistake. All are discussed below. However, the elements that comprise these grounds are often difficult to prove.

a. Fraud

Fraud or misrepresentation occurs when a salesman is given false promises about his working arrangement that induce him to work for the company. All of the following factors must be proved:

1. Important and specific promises must be given to the salesman;

2. Stated by company officials who knew that they were false with the intention that the salesman would rely upon them;

3. Believed to be true by the salesman;

4. Who then entered into a contract in reliance upon these promises; and

5. Suffered injury as a result.

Fraud can be illustrated by the following hypothetical situation. A company representative tells you that you will have exclusive territorial rights in certain states. This representation is false, but you have no way of checking it. Believing the company's representations to be true, you orally agree to begin working for it. You may have good grounds to rescind your contract once you discover that another salesman is working in your territory.

If you think that you can prove all of the above elements and you elect to rescind your contract, you should do so when you discover the fraud. If you wait too long, a court may declare that you lost your opportunity to rescind.

b. Mistake

Contracts can be rescinded if they are entered into as a result of a mistaken belief. This ignorance must involve an important fact that did not result from a person's failure to pay proper attention and use good business judgment.

All salesmen have a legal duty to investigate the matters and details of their working arrangement. They cannot allege mistake whenever they feel like it in order to free themselves from their contract. For example, if you fail to read your written contract before you sign it, you cannot claim mistake in order to obtain a rescission.

c. Duress

If proven, duress will give you a valid reason to rescind your contract. This occurs when a person is the victim of a threat that deprives him of his freedom of will not to enter into a contract or perform certain tasks. Threats of physical harm constitute duress. For example, if a salesman was told that he would be fired unless he went down the street and stole a competitor's machine, this would constitute duress. Salesmen should contact an attorney immediately if they are being subjected to such pressures.

4. Rescission by Court Decree

After reading this book you should question all unfair provisions in your employment contract. However, if you enter into an agreement that is one-sided, a court may rescind the contract if it determines that it is grossly unfair. A court will look to the facts surrounding the making of the contract and the provisions contained within it.

Helpful Hints

If a company offers you a written contract and gives you no opportunity to negotiate its terms (on a "take it or leave it" basis) and you sign it, see a lawyer at once if you think that its provisions:

1. Are grossly unfair;

2. Differ markedly from standard contracts entered into by other salesmen within your industry; and

3. Include some "surprise" clauses that you did not understand when signing your contract.

REMEDIES FOR BREACH OF CONTRACT

SECTION 11
BREACH OF CONTRACT

This chapter will discuss the legal consequences that arise after contracts of employment have been breached.

A. WHAT IS A BREACH OF A CONTRACT?

A breach of contract occurs when terms of the contract are not followed. This may result from either party's failure to perform obligations agreed upon in the contract or when either party does acts that the contract expressly prohibits. Unless there is a legal excuse to justify actions that violate the terms of a contract, a salesman or his company will be viewed as being in breach.

B. WHAT DAMAGES ARE AVAILABLE FOR THE BREACH OF A CONTRACT?

If a salesman or company breaches the contract, damages may be awarded to the injured party. The injured party is the person who did *not* breach the contract. Damages are amounts of money that the court awards to satisfy someone for the injury suffered. A court will not award damages unless the amount can be reasonably calculated. Therefore, a salesman should always keep careful records of his sales and accounts so that it will be possible to estimate the damages he should receive (note that speculation is not a sufficient basis to award damages).

A salesman or his company is usually awarded one of the following kinds of damages when a contract has been breached:

1. Compensatory Damages

This type of damage is most frequently awarded to a salesman when he sues his company. It is designed to put the injured salesman in the same position he would have been in if the terms of his contract had been performed. This amount may also include money for future lost profits which would have resulted had the contract not been breached. Thus, if a salesman was fired without notice yet was entitled to sixty days' notice by the terms of his contract, he would be allowed to recover the salary and his estimated commissions for the sixty-day period.

2. Nominal Damages

This is money given to an injured party who is technically in the right but suffers only a small harm. The amount of money received is always very small, that is, $1.00. Some unfortunate salesmen who are unable to properly estimate their damages in court (often because of poor record keeping) are awarded this amount.

3. Liquidated Damages

This is a predetermined amount of money that the injured party will receive when the contract is breached. Liquidated damages are discussed more fully in a later section of this chapter.

C. COMMON EXAMPLES INVOLVING BREACH OF CONTRACT

This section will examine a number of occasions when the salesman or his company breaches their contract.

1. Wrongful Termination by the Company
a. What is a wrongful termination?

Whether you have been wrongfully terminated depends upon the type of agreement you have with your company.

1. *Hired at will:* A salesman is hired at will when his job may be terminated anytime at his option or at the option of the company. Many salesmen are hired this way. If you were hired at will, it is highly unlikely that you can be wrongfully terminated, since the company can terminate you *with* or *without reason.*

2. *Hired subject to notice:* Many salesmen, even those hired at will, have a clause in their contract that states that they can be terminated only if they are given advance notice. This notice usually ranges anywhere from thirty days to one year. If you have been terminated without advance notice, it is likely that you have been wrongfully terminated.

3. *Hired for a specified period:* Some salesmen are hired for a specified period (usually one year). If the company seeks to terminate you before the year has ended, you will have been wrongfully terminated unless your company has good cause to fire you.

b. When can you sue for wrongful termination?

You can sue the company when:

1. You are formally terminated; or

2. The company's actions indicate that you are no longer employed by the company; or

3. The company's actions make it intolerable for a normal salesman to work and you quit. Even if you sign a voluntary letter of resignation, you may still sue the company if its actions made it impossible for you to perform your selling duties.

c. Remedies for the salesman

If you have been terminated, you will be entitled to collect damages from the company. If you were:

1. *Hired at will:* You will probably receive nothing,

since it is very difficult to prove wrongful termination.

2. *Hired subject to notice:* You will be entitled to all salary and commissions that you earn from the time that you were notified of the firing to the time called for in the notice period. Thus, if your contract calls for ninety days' notice and you are only given ten days' notice before termination, you are entitled to all salary and commissions that could reasonably have been earned in the next eighty days. If you are fired without notice, you can generally collect damages for the notice period. This is ninety days in the previous example.

3. *Hired for a specified period:* You will be entitled to all salary and commissions that could reasonably have been earned from the time you were fired to the termination date. Thus, if you were hired for a one-year term and terminated twenty-six weeks later, you would be entitled to all salary and commissions that you reasonably could have earned in the next twenty-six weeks.

The court will determine the amount of commissions you could have earned. Thus, you should try to keep your past sales records as accurate as possible since they will be helpful to the court in determining the amount of your claim. During the lawsuit your attorney may be entitled to examine the company's prior sales records for your territory and product. This information may also form a basis for your damages.

If you are selling for an unestablished business, it will be very difficult for the court to determine what sales could have been made if the contract had not been breached. As a result, a claim for damages based on anticipated sales would be very hard to prove, since the damages would be speculative.

d. Duties of the salesman

In order to collect damages from your company, there are a number of things you must do before a court will award you money. Failure to do any of the following after you have been terminated will result in a *reduction* of damages.

1. *Mitigation of damages.* You must make an attempt to get another job if you want to collect *all* the damages you are entitled to. This concept is referred to as mitigation of dam-

ages. If you do not make a good faith attempt to get another job, a court will reduce your company's remaining payment obligation by the amount you *could* have earned had you made such efforts. If employment is available in a similar line of work with comparable rate of salary and is located near your place of prior employment, you have a duty to accept this job. However, a chemical salesman is under no obligation to accept a job as an insurance salesman. Similarly, you would not be expected to move from New York to Chicago to accept a job.

If you obtain another job, the income that you earn may be used to offset your damage recovery. If you do not secure employment but have made reasonable efforts to obtain a similar job, you will be entitled to all damages under the terms of your contract. It is also possible to recover money for the expenses you reasonably incurred while seeking other employment in your effort to mitigate damages. If you do get another job and earn income in excess of your damages, you will not recover damages from the company. Of course, you will not owe the company for the excess earned.

2. *Offers of reemployment.* If your company makes an offer to reemploy you in the same or a similar position and you do not accept, the company may not have to pay you damages for money that you lost after this offer of reemployment.

If your company offers to reemploy you but tells you that various provisions in your employment contract will be changed or that you will be offered a different position, you do not have to accept the offer of reemployment. If your relationship with the company has deteriorated to the point where further association with it is offensive or degrading, or if you have accepted another offer of employment from a different company, you can generally *reject* your company's offer of reemployment.

If you accept a new and different position with your company, you have rescinded (nullified) your old contract (see Section 10). By doing so, you have surrendered your claim for breach of the original contract.

2. Wrongful Termination by the Salesman
a. What is wrongful termination?

Whether you have wrongfully terminated your contract again depends upon your particular agreement. If you were:

1. *Hired at will:* You can generally leave your job at any time.

2. *Hired subject to notice:* You may leave if proper notice was given.

3. *Hired for a specified period:* You may leave your job at the end of the period or during the term if the company neglects to perform certain material duties. Material duties include the company's failure to pay commissions, refusal to honor territorial rights arrangements, or failure to ship your orders.

b. Remedies for the company

Salesmen may be required to pay damages when they leave their jobs earlier than their contracts specify, and courts assess damages that are owed. There is no set formula for determining how much money is to be paid, and the method for determining damages depends upon the particular facts of each case.

The following are some of the types of damages that salesmen have been required to pay:

1. The company can recover the money it spent in its efforts to obtain your replacement for the remainder of the employment term. This may involve subtracting the difference of what the company had to pay a new salesman from what it paid you; or

2. Damages based upon the following factors:

a. The loss of patronage occurring after you left the business;

b. The company's need for your services;

c. The peculiar value of your services;

d. The harm done when you begin working for a rival company.

These factors can cause you to lose a substantial amount of money if you wrongfully terminate your employment contract. Even if you lose benefits such as pension, insurance, and retirement plans, this will not relieve you of your responsibility to pay damages if the contract was breached.

c. How to protect yourself from a lawsuit

You can protect yourself if you have wrongfully terminated your contract by having your company sign a waiver. When a waiver is signed, the company agrees to treat the contract as being canceled. This relinquishes any claims against you for breach of the contract. The following is an example of a waiver:

> The (Company) *hereby Waives the breach of the contract by* (Salesman) *in addition to Waiving all rights or remedies at law or in equity for the breach it may have.*

If your company voluntarily allows you to breach your contract, obtain the above waiver in writing. A written waiver protects you if the company later changes its mind and decides to sue.

3. Company's Failure to Pay Commissions

If the company breaches your contract by failing to pay money that is due, a court will award you damages for the amount that is unpaid, plus interest.

4. Company's Failure to Honor Territorial Rights

If you have an exclusive territory and the company assigns part of your territory to another salesman despite your objections, the company will have breached your contract. Generally, you can recover damages for the amount of commissions you have been deprived of as a result of the company's actions. It is *vital* for you to obtain a record of all company sales so that you can determine how much you are owed.

5. Salesman's Breach of Duty of Loyalty

A salesman owes his company a duty of loyalty. This duty is violated if the salesman establishes a competing business while working for the company, or if he intentionally steers customers to another company. If such conduct can be proved, the salesman will have breached his duty of loyalty and can be sued by the company for lost profits resulting from his actions. In addition, the salesman is *not* entitled to payment of commissions if he performs acts that are disloyal to the company.

6. Salesman's Breach of the Covenant Not to Compete

If a salesman signs a contract that prohibits him from competing with his company for a certain period of time, the salesman will have breached his contract if he works for a competing company during the time period specified in his original contract. Usually courts do not require the salesman to pay money damages. Rather, they order him to stop competing for a specified period. However, when a salesman is required to pay damages, the company is usually compensated for lost profits. This amount can be quite substantial. (See Section 8 for an explanation of your options if you desire to breach the covenant.)

D. LIQUIDATED DAMAGES PROVISIONS

1. What Is a Liquidated Damages Provision?

A liquidated damages provision is a clause that specifies in advance the consequences that will result once a breach of contract occurs. It can be written for either the benefit of the salesman or his company and usually provides that the party guilty of the breach will pay the other party a specified amount of money. These provisions are easy to recognize because they usually contain a dollar figure that must be paid if there is a breach of contract. Note that the words "liquidated damages" need not be specifically mentioned.

Liquidated damages provisions are usually allowed by the courts if:

a. The injury caused by the breach is difficult or impossible to estimate; for example, determining a salesman's future commission earnings;

    b. The amount specified will be compensation for damages and will not serve as a penalty; and

    c. The amount to be paid is a reasonable estimate of the probable loss.

2. Examples of Liquidated Damages Provisions

The following is an example of a liquidated damages clause drafted for the benefit of the company:

> *If the Sales Representative breaches the terms of this employment agreement, he shall pay to the Company the sum of $X as liquidated damages since it is impossible to calculate the exact cost or injury that the Company may sustain by reason of the breach, and such sum is not a penalty.*

A salesman who breached his contract would have to pay the company the dollar figure specified in the liquidated damages provision.

A salesman may also desire a liquidated damages provision in the event that his contract is breached. An example of such a provision follows:

> *In the event that the Company violates this contract of service by dismissing the Salesman without just cause before the end of the term, the Company agrees to pay the sum of $X as liquidated damages, since it is impossible to calculate the injury that the Salesman may sustain by reason of the breach, and such sum is not a penalty.*

A liquidated damages provision similar to the above allows full recovery should the company breach the contract. If you obtain such a clause, your damages are fixed by the contract and you do not have to seek other employment in order to collect damages.

3. Do You Want a Liquidated Damages Provision?

The advantage of a liquidated damages provision is that both the company and the salesman are fully aware of the damages to be awarded after the contract has been breached. Salesmen should accept this arrangement when the damages he may have to pay are minimal.

Conversely, a salesman should insist upon a liquidated damages provision that awards him significant damages.

SECTION 12
UNJUST ENRICHMENT

A. WHAT IS UNJUST ENRICHMENT?

When a salesman spends his own money and devotes his time and labor for a company, the law allows him to recover for his efforts. He may sell goods, answer telephones, or help in promotional activities several weeks before his contract is to begin and for one reason or another never start to formally work for the company. On the other hand, he may be asked to perform duties even after he is no longer working.

In both of these instances, once the company receives an economic benefit, the salesman *must* be paid for the *reasonable* value of his efforts. This legal remedy is referred to as *quantum meruit*, and courts will enforce it in order to prevent unjust enrichment at the salesman's expense. This section will explore situations where salesmen can use this remedy to their advantage.

B. WHEN ARE YOU ENTITLED TO MONEY FOR SERVICES?

In order to recover compensation, you must be able to prove in court the following four elements:

1. That you did something and/or expended money that *benefitted* the company;

2. That you did this *expecting* to be paid for these services;

3. That you were asked to perform these tasks and did *not* volunteer your services; and

4. That it would be *unfair* to have the company retain the value of these services and not pay you for them.

Take the following recent case for example. A salesman was working for a hardware company on a commission basis. His job was to locate various construction projects, secure plans for building construction, prepare lists of the hardware required, and submit his company's bid. If the bid was accepted, he then had to supervise timely delivery to the job and resolve all disputes between his company and the purchaser of the hardware. His contract stated that commissions for his services were not to be paid until his company had been paid in full. The salesman did all of these tasks faithfully and resigned after the company refused to pay him commissions. The company had received only $6,000 from one $9,000 order and argued that it did not have to pay its salesman his commissions since the company had not been paid in full. The court ruled that even though the contract stated otherwise, the salesman was entitled, under an unjust enrichment theory, to the reasonable value of the services that he performed.

If you have a contract and are asked to perform *additional* work, you cannot recover more money unless the work was different from your usual duties and the company promised that you would be paid for this extra work. Companies often defeat unjust enrichment claims after demonstrating that it was reasonable for them to expect that they would not have to pay the salesman, particularly when similar companies in the industry did not pay additional money for this kind of work.

You can only recover if you do something at the request, permission, and insistence of the company. If you volunteer to do something, for example, to "show your stuff" in the hope that the company will recognize your talents, your claim for payment will fail.

Helpful Hints

If you no longer work for a company but are requested to do some additional work for which you will be paid, insist that the company put this promise in writing.

If the company makes a commitment to hire you and you spend your own money for advertising, promotion, showroom fees, telephone calls to new accounts, etc., in the anticipation that you will be working for the company and it then tells you that your services are not required, do not hesitate to either consult an attorney or sue in Small Claims Court to recover these expenses. *Always* keep accurate records so that you can prove these expenses in court.

If a company official requests that you do additional work for which you will be paid, have him specify your duties and rate of compensation. Be certain that the official is in an authorized position to make such an offer and bind the company.

THE SALESMAN'S LEGAL OPTIONS

SECTION 13
DISPUTES WITH THE COMPANY

A. IT'S TIME TO TAKE A STAND!

When a salesman and his company have a dispute, the problem is usually corrected long before the salesman begins to contemplate taking legal action. Through give-and-take the dispute is usually ironed out. However, many times the problem has not been resolved to the satisfaction of the salesman and he simply accepts a bad situation and learns to live with it. He may feel that instituting a lawsuit will harm his reputation in the trade. Or he may believe that since he is making a comfortable living with the company it is wise not to create trouble and risk losing his job. This type of thinking will enable his company to continue cheating the salesman out of money that rightfully belongs to him.

B. WHY LITIGATION?

Your career as a salesman will not end once you begin litigation. On the contrary, thousands of salesmen have instituted lawsuits and are currently very successful in their fields. If you are a salesman who works hard and has established a reputation with accounts in your territory, any honest employer will not be intimidated by the fact that you have instituted suit against another company. For one thing, blacklisting is an illegal restraint of trade. Additionally, your new employer wants to receive the sales from the accounts that you will bring to his company. Finally, you are protecting your reputation with your accounts as a "no-nonsense" salesman who lives by his word and will fight for what he believes is right. Your customers have to respect you for taking such a stand. Remember, you are not asking for anything that you do not legally deserve. Having lived up to your terms of the agreement, you are asking your employer to live up to his obligations.

The decision to litigate is not as earth-shattering as you may have been led to believe. Being legally informed, you know what your rights are. What you have discovered by accident may be the tip of the iceberg. Only a lawsuit can compel the production of the company's documents, records, invoices, accounts receivable, and shipping lists. From these records it is often discovered that you are owed far more money than you originally thought. If your employer has been cheating you, he may wish to settle out of court shortly after receiving your complaint for breach of contract. Or, chances are that he may settle the matter prior to turning over his documents for your inspection.

C. PREPARATION FOR A LAWSUIT

If you feel that you have been subjected to injustices that can only be resolved in a courtroom, it is wise to begin looking for a new job before taking legal action. Resort to litigation or arbitration will probably result in the termination of your job, since the mutual trust and respect required for a solid working relationship will have ceased. Do not expect to be able to go back to work for the company once your case has been resolved. Do not expect to continue carrying its product while the suit progresses. Plan ahead. Look for a replacement line several months in advance of the commencement of your suit. Try to time the commencement of your suit several weeks before the beginning of a new selling season so that when you are terminated you will be able to start your new job off on the right foot.

Most written contracts provide that the salesman may carry additional lines with the full knowledge of the company provided that additional lines do not compete. Standard trade practice often allows you to look for other lines while working. You may do this, but be inconspicuous. Do not publicize the fact that you are seeking a new product line to replace your old one. This may enable your company to contend that you did not exercise the required *good faith* while working for them. You may also be subjecting yourself to the argument that the replacement line was a competing line and that you obtained it in violation of the terms of your agreement. Be careful. Remember, you are still considered to be in your company's employ until your contract has actually been terminated.

The following sections will discuss the various types of legal recourse that salesmen can utilize. The advantages and disadvantages of each form will be analyzed at length.

SECTION 14
OUT-OF-COURT SETTLEMENTS

When a dispute arises between a salesman and his company, the problem may be resolved by means of an out-of-court settlement. This need not involve the use of a lawyer. The most frequently used method to resolve disputes is referred to as an accord and satisfaction. An accord is an agreement to settle a dispute and a satisfaction results when the company pays the salesman the amount of money that has been agreed upon. This process allows salesmen to receive their money quickly and avoid legal expense. To obtain a valid accord and satisfaction the following conditions must be met:

1. There must be a disputed claim;
2. There will be an offer of a lesser amount of money in full settlement of the claim; and
3. The salesman will accept the lesser amount in satisfaction of the debt.

In essence, an accord and satisfaction is a compromise. Once the salesman and company agree to a valid accord and satisfaction, the salesman cannot collect the balance of the money that he believes is owed to him. For example, if the salesman claims he is owed $1,000 and the company contends he is only owed $500, the salesman and the company may agree that $750 will be sufficient to satisfy the claim in full. Once they agree to this amount and the salesman is paid, he cannot subsequently sue the company in an attempt to collect the additional $250.

A. ENTERING INTO AN ACCORD AND SATISFACTION

If there is a *disputed* claim and an accord and satisfaction is desired, *both* the salesman and the company must agree that payment is in *full* satisfaction of the debt. An accord and satisfaction can be easily accomplished. Usually, the company will simply mail the salesman a check that is marked "balance for commissions" or "payment in full." In other cases, language on the back of a check may state the following:

> *Endorsement and payment of this check constitutes a full release by the Salesman of all claims for commissions or otherwise against the Company and its affiliates.*

When you endorse and cash a check that contains this type of language, the accord and satisfaction becomes binding. The company is released from any claims that you have concerning this debt and you cannot sue it to collect additional money.

B. ACCORD AND SATISFACTION WHERE THE DEBT IS NOT DISPUTED

The law usually requires a valid dispute concerning the amount of money owed for there to be an accord and satisfaction. If there is *no* dispute, courts in many states will not allow the company to pay the salesman a lesser amount in full satisfaction of the debt. Thus, if you were owed $2,000 and your company sent you a check for $1,000 marked "payment in full," which you cashed, there would be no accord and satisfaction and the company would still owe you $1,000.

However, all salesmen should contact an attorney to discover how their state treats partial payment of undisputed debts. Some states have enacted laws that say that partial payment of a debt will satisfy the entire debt if a person accepts partial payment in *writing*. In these states, if you endorse a check accompanied by a letter that tells you the check has been sent to "close your account," or cash a check marked "payment in full," you will be unable to collect the balance. However, *oral* agreements to settle for a lesser amount of an undisputed claim will *not* bind you.

Helpful Hints

If your claim is *not* disputed:

1. Be certain that both you and the company agree about the amount owed.

2. Learn how the law in your state treats accord and satisfaction and undisputed claims.

3. If the law in your state does *not* recognize an accord and satisfaction of an undisputed claim, you *may* want to cash your company's check and sue for the balance. By cashing the check, you obtain some of the money immediately. The rest may have to be recovered via a lawsuit.

4. If the law in your state *does* recognize an accord and satisfaction of an undisputed claim, do *not* cash the check unless you want to settle the claim.

C. ACCORD AND SATISFACTION WHERE THE DEBT IS DISPUTED

If your claim is disputed do *not* cash the check unless you want to settle. Many salesmen try to "outsmart" their companies by crossing out the words "payment in full" and writing in words to the effect that the check is only a partial payment for the debt. Many courts have ruled that once you cash the check, you have accepted it as *full payment* and no longer have a claim against the company.

If you do not want to settle, you should *return* the

check to your company. In some states, if you hold the check for an unreasonable amount of time without cashing it and without indicating that it has been refused, you will be deemed to have *accepted* the check in satisfaction of your debt. Thus, for your own safety, *return* the check and indicate that you have refused the company's offer.

Salesmen should *never* agree to settle unless they have sufficient information regarding the amount of money that is owed to them. For example, if $500 is owed but you have reason to suspect that additional money may be due, demand to see the company's books. If the company owes you thousands of dollars but you agree to settle by cashing a check for $500, you probably will be unable to collect the balance. However, if the company purposely deceives you about the amount of money that is owed, you can sue for the balance despite the fact that you agreed to an accord and satisfaction.

SECTION 15
ARBITRATION

Arbitration is an alternative to formal litigation whereby disputes are settled without resorting to the court system. Cases are resolved by arbitrators who are not bound to make their decisions using strict rules of legal procedure. Since arbitration differs markedly from civil litigation, both the salesman and the company must mutually agree upon the arbitration process.

A. METHODS OF OBTAINING ARBITRATION

1. Submission Agreements
The decision to arbitrate may arise in one of two situations. The first instance usually occurs at the time when the dispute has crystallized. Both sides agree that they cannot resolve their differences themselves and that their problems will be submitted to arbitration. A "Submission Agreement" is then signed. Such a document identifies both the salesman

and his company as parties in the dispute, states that the dispute is to be settled by arbitration, describes what both parties wish to obtain in damages, and discusses the rules to be employed in the selection of arbitrators.

Submission Agreements rarely cause any problems when signed since the desire to submit to arbitration is not in dispute. However, if the company or salesman then commences an action by filing a complaint in court, *both* parties forfeit their right to arbitration. The right to arbitrate is considered waived and the Submission Agreement has no effect.

2. Contractual Provision

An agreement to arbitrate may also be contained in a contract. A typical arbitration clause in an employment contract between a salesman and his company will state the following:

> *Any claim or controversy arising among or between the parties hereto and any claim or controversy arising out of or respecting any matter contained in this Agreement or any differences as to the interpretation of any of the provisions of this Agreement shall be settled by* arbitration *in this city by three (3) arbitrators under the prevailing rules of the American Arbitration Association. The award of the arbitrators shall be final and binding.*

When such a provision is used, both parties relinquish their right to sue in court and agree to submit future disputes to the binding decision of arbitrators.

A written agreement to arbitrate future disputes is enforceable in many states including New York, Florida, California, and Massachusetts. However, salesmen should be aware that the decision to arbitrate future disputes must be in *writing.* This rule is quite strict. Some states even require that the document must be signed in order to be enforceable. Thus, salesmen should consult with an attorney if they desire arbitration and must remember that an oral agreement to arbitrate will *not* be honored.

If your written contract contains an arbitration clause

that gives either party the *option* to arbitrate or litigate, the clause will not be valid. Both parties must be bound if the clause is to have any legal effect. In addition, salesmen are reminded that if they sign a contract that states that they will be bound by the rules of arbitration contained in another agreement, they should read the other document. To avoid the claim that one of the parties was unaware of the arbitration procedures to be followed, or that he was unfairly relinquishing his access to the courts, both parties should initial the other document and attach a copy of it to the original contract.

B. ADVANTAGES OF ARBITRATION

The process of arbitration works far more quickly and cheaply than litigation. It may take a civil case four years to be resolved, while the same case in arbitration might take four months from the date of filing the complaint to the day of decision. Those salesman who are seeking a quick resolution of their problem should take this factor into account. In addition, there is far less preparation for an arbitration case than a full trial. The average arbitration lasts less than a day in comparison to a trial, which may last several days. If you are paying attorney fees by the hour or by the hour plus a flat per-day court rate, as opposed to contingency fees (see Section 17), the arbitration route affords you considerable savings. Also, many people favor arbitration because the arbitrators who are selected are usually familiar with the trade practices in your industry. This reduces court time because they are able to "trim the fat" and concentrate on the contractual provisions in dispute.

C. DISADVANTAGES OF ARBITRATION

An agreement to arbitrate is essentially a decision to surrender many of the protections a salesman has at his disposal when litigating in court. The process of arbitrator selection is viewed with suspicion in instances where each party picks his own arbitrator, since it is assumed that one of the arbitrators is already more sympathetic to one side or the other. In addition, arbitration is a private proceeding. Arbitrators, unlike judges, need not give formal reasons for their decisions. In most cases there is no formal record of the proceeding. This eliminates your right to appeal for all practical purposes and gives you the right to obtain an appeal only in the unusual instances of arbitrator partiality or misconduct.

Arbitrators have a free hand to decide what evidence they will listen to in order to justify their findings. Unlike judges, they may wish not to decide the case on the precedent of past decisions, and some states do not even require that an oath be administered before testimony is taken.

D. PRACTICAL REASONS AGAINST ARBITRATION

At the time when arbitration is contemplated, you should contact an attorney if your company tells you that arbitration should be agreed upon as the method for settling disputes. The initial cost of instituting legal action will be approximately the same. With arbitration or litigation, you will have to hire an attorney, possibly pay him a fee for the initial interview, and advance him a retainer. Before the arbitration process begins, your attorney must file a complaint against the company in roughly the same detail as he would if it were a court case.

Salesmen may wish to avoid arbitration for the following reasons:

Loss of Discovery Rights

If you opt for arbitration you may lose your most important weapon, that is, the right to view your company's private records. In most states, the pre-trial discovery procedures available to a court are either limited or eliminated by arbitration. For example, devices such as interrogatories, depositions, and notices to produce documents for inspection will, absent extraordinary circumstances, not be ordered by a court once the arbitrators have been selected. The arbitrators then have the power to decide what company records and documents they will view. Their decision is discretionary and a salesman's request to view company books may be denied on the basis that his request is a fishing expedition designed to upset company operations.

If company records are brought to the arbitration hearing, a salesman and his attorney may have neither the time nor the means to determine whether the records are complete and/or accurate and will have no choice but to ask for a continuance. If the company fails to bring in requested records on the day of the hearing, the arbitrators do not have the authority to hold company officials in contempt, although they can take this conduct into account when determining an award.

These factors suggest that although pretrial discovery is often expensive, it is warranted in cases where the salesman believes a substantial amount of money has been withheld from him. Without such records it is impossible to discover the true dollar amount of goods shipped into the salesman's territory and the sales made at the company's showroom for salesmen who travel "on the road."

Stricter Enforcement of Trade Customs

Companies favor no-nonsense arbitrators who are aware of the trade meaning of the contract terms and are knowledgeable as to the various aspects of performance arising from these terms. For example, there is disagreement among salesmen and companies in the apparel industry whether the 85 percent guaranteed shipping clause is enforceable. This means that an arbitrator may tend to disallow it while a judge would be more likely to view the failure to conform to the 85 percent figure as a breach by the company of an important contract term.

Loss of Sympathetic Juries

The arbitrators who are selected are usually successful businessmen and attorneys. Their philosophical orientation may be more closely aligned with the company. Juries, however, are generally sympathetic to the everyday problems that salesmen experience in their trade. This is an important factor to consider. Additionally, your company is knowledgeable about arbitration procedures and strategies if they have been to arbitration before. If so, you can minimize the company's experience by taking them to court.

E. Removal to Arbitration

The technical aspects of arbitration procedure, including filing, will not be discussed in this work, because the services of an attorney will be required after the decision to arbitrate is made. However, since arbitration procedure varies markedly from state to state, a lawyer should always be consulted when the decision to arbitrate is being *considered*. In addition, the following point should be remembered by salesmen who institute suit in New York City against their companies. If you commence a lawsuit in court and claim damages below $6,000, a judge has the power to remove the case and have it decided by a panel of arbitrators. Not all cases under $6,000 are removed to arbitration. The decision lies in the judge's discretion. However, once a judge places the case in arbitration, his decision is final even if neither party wishes to arbitrate. After the case is heard, the losing party may request a new civil trial provided he makes this request within thirty days of the filing of the arbitration award. However, he must pay approximately $150, which includes court costs and payment for the arbitrators' services.

SECTION 16
SMALL CLAIMS COURT

Small Claims Courts enable salesmen and other employees to litigate their claims in an informal and inexpensive manner. The advantage of Small Claims Court is that it is not necessary to hire an attorney to handle your case. However, it is surprising to note that many individuals are unaware of the existence of Small Claims Courts and fail to use them to their maximum advantage. Thus, the following material should be read carefully in order to gain valuable insights about this method of legal recourse.

A. SITUATIONS WHERE SMALL CLAIMS COURT IS HELPFUL

After working several months for a company, Gil, an independent selling agent, decides that the operation does not suit him and he properly terminates his working relationship. However, the company owes several hundred dollars in commissions, which it refuses to pay. Gil is told to sell his sample line if he wishes to recover this money. However, Gil believes this is unfair because additional effort and expense will be required and he may not be able to recover all of the money he is owed. Since this was not the arrangement that he and his company orally agreed upon, Gil wishes to return the line as originally promised and receive his money. Thus, he should not hesitate to resolve this dispute in Small Claims Court.

Small Claims Court should not be utilized merely in contractual disputes. Small Claims Court can help you if your property is damaged and the person who caused the damage will not repair or replace it. Or a landlord may promise to return your security deposit but later fails to do so. You may buy merchandise that is damaged during delivery and the store refuses to replace and/or return it. In all of these cases, and countless more, you should sue in Small Claims Court to recover your loss.

The information contained below describes the procedures of a typical Small Claims Court. However, the courts in each city and state are often quite different. Thus, before you begin suit in a particular Small Claims Court, it is wise to call the clerk of that court and ask for an explanation of the specific rules to be followed.

B. WHO MAY BE SUED?

A Small Claims Court may be used to sue any person, business, or corporation who owes you money. However, Small Claims Courts have a maximum limit for money that you can sue for and recover if you are successful. This figure usually ranges from $300 to $1,500. If you sue in Small Claims Court and recover a judgment, you are precluded from suing again to recover any additional money owed to you. Thus, if you feel that your claim greatly exceeds the maximum amount of money that might be awarded in Small Claims Court, you may wish to institute suit in a municipal or district court. In this event, you will need a lawyer.

C. WHERE TO BRING SUIT

Call your local Bar Association to discover where the Small Claims Courts are located. You cannot sue in the location of your choice. Usually, suit can only be brought in the city or town where the *defendant* lives or does business. Check with the clerk about this. Also, inquire what hours the court is in session (for example, evening sessions are held in New York City Small Claims Courts) and whether it is necessary to fill the forms out personally before the clerk or whether this may be done by mail.

D. WHAT YOU CAN SUE FOR

You can sue only to collect *money* that you believe is rightfully owed to you. If, for example, you believe that you are entitled to samples that were paid for but not received by you, or for additional services that you performed for your company and were not reimbursed for, you must estimate the loss in money that you wish to collect. All amounts should include additional unreimbursed out-of-pocket expenses accompanied by written receipts.

E. THE SUIT IS STARTED

1. Filing a Complaint
You begin the suit by paying a small fee (about $3.00) and stating on a complaint presented to you by the clerk:

a. Your name and address;

b. The full name and address of the person or corporation you are suing;

c. The facts and reasons why you have brought this claim; and

d. The money you believe you are rightfully owed.

These statements do not have to be elaborate and formal. It is usually sufficient to write that the defendant is indebted to you for a specified amount, that a demand for payment has been made to him, and that he has refused to pay. In addition, be certain to state the defendant's complete and accurate name and address so that you will not have difficulty obtaining money if you are awarded a judgment. (Note: Before beginning the suit you should contact the proper state agency, such as the Secretary of State's office, to obtain the corporation's full name and address.)

The following is an example of a simple complaint:

I work for X Company on a commission basis. At the end of my employment term, X Company owed me $450 in commissions. Demand for payment was made repeatedly and X Company has refused to pay. This action is commenced to recover the $450 that X Company rightfully owes me.

At this time you will also fill out a summons, which will be sent to the defendant by certified mail. This will notify him of the suit and inform him of the hearing date. For a typical case in Manhattan, New York, the interim period from the date of filing to the trial is approximately one month.

2. The Defendant's Response

When the defendant receives the summons, he or his attorney can counterclaim, deny by personally appearing in court on the day of the hearing, or write a denial and mail it to the court. If a written denial is mailed to the court, you should request the clerk to recite the denial over the phone or else go down to the court and read it yourself. This is your right and it will help you prepare for your opponent's defense. The following is an example of a simple denial in an answer:

I deny each and every allegation on the face of the complaint.

This denial causes the plaintiff to prove his charges in court.

3. Your Duties

If you are the moving party in the suit, that is, the plaintiff, you have a duty to carefully follow the progress of the case. Refer your case to the clerk by the *docket number* and check to see that the defendant received the summons and/or answered the complaint. If you discover that the defendant has not received the summons by the day of the trial, ask the clerk to have it *personally served* by a sheriff and find out how many days it must be served on him before the new trial date. Once a summons has been received and the defendant does not appear at the trial, he will default and you will automatically be awarded the judgment. However, this may not occur if there was a good reason why the defendant did not appear and his motion to remove the default judgment is accepted by the court. If this judgment is granted, the trial will be rescheduled for a new date. If the defendant is not a corporation, you may have to file a Military Affidavit which states that the defendant is not in the service and serving overseas.

If you cannot be present on the date of the trial, send a certified letter to the clerk explaining your reasons and ask for a *continuance*. Include future dates when you know you can appear. Call the clerk the day before the old trial date to make sure that your request has been granted and that the case will not be dismissed against you. Also, check to see that the defendant is in receipt of a letter informing him of the revised trial date.

4. Preparing for Trial

When preparing for the trial, be certain that all of your friendly witnesses, if any, will attend the trial and testify on your behalf. If necessary, ask the clerk to issue a subpoena to

compel the attendance of key disinterested witnesses who refuse to voluntarily attend and testify at the hearing. Unfortunately, people who tell you they will appear do not always do
so. Therefore, it is best to subpoena all important witnesses.

F. THE TRIAL

On the day of the trial, arrive early, find your name on the
court calendar, and check in with the clerk. Come prepared
with all relevant documents, shipping lists, commission statements, accounts receivable lists, bills, receipts, canceled
checks, employment contracts, copies of certified letters, and
signed affidavits. Wait until your case is called. You and the
other party will then be sworn in. The judge will conduct the
hearing and ask you questions. Be relaxed, state your case,
and show the judge your records. Bring along a short written
summary of your case. You can refer to it during the trial and
in the event that the judge does not come to an immediate decision but rather takes the case under *advisement*, he can refer
to your outline.

　　After both sides have finished speaking, you then have
the opportunity to refute what your opponent has told the
judge. Do not become alarmed if he is accompanied by an attorney (some courts do not allow lawyers to participate, others actively discourage their use). Simply inform the judge in
a polite tone that you are not represented by counsel and are
not familiar with Small Claims Court procedure. Ask the
judge to intercede on your behalf if you feel that your opponent's attorney is treating you unfairly. Most judges will be
sympathetic, since Small Claims Courts are specifically designed so that you can present your case without an attorney
being present. In addition, always question procedures that
are unfamiliar to you.

G. OBTAINING JUDGMENT

If you win the case, make sure that you know how and when
payment will be made. If the defendant has not complied with

the order to pay you, you may then petition for notice to show cause. This will be sent to the defendant asking him to come into court and explain why he has not paid.

Once you start proceedings in Small Claims Court, you waive your right to a jury. However, the defendant can surprise you. Some states allow defendants to remove a Small Claims Court case to a higher court and/or later obtain a trial by jury. If this occurs, you will need a lawyer, and his services could conceivably cost as much as your claim in the dispute.

SECTION 17
LITIGATION

Once a salesman has decided that the problem with his company requires legal attention and there are sufficiently complex legal problems that cannot be handled in Small Claims Court, he must speak with an attorney in order to properly evaluate and act upon his claim. Lawyers should be selected with utmost care. You should be represented by a competent practitioner who will protect your interests and reasonably bill you for services. If you have dealt with an attorney in the past and have confidence in his abilities, do not hesitate to call him for the purpose of scheduling an appointment. If you do not have an attorney, ask relatives and friends if they can recommend someone. Most attorneys receive clients in this fashion. In addition, you may also wish to contact your local Bar Association and ask for the names of attorneys who specialize in contract law.

A. THE INITIAL INTERVIEW

At the initial interview, bring all pertinent written information (employment contracts, letters of intent, company memoranda, shipping lists, invoices, commission statements, etc.) with you. Tell the attorney everything related to your problem, since all such communications made to him are privileged and this will save time and make it easier for him to assess your case.

Once your lawyer receives all of the pertinent facts, he will then:

1. Decide whether your case has a fair probability of success after considering the law in the state where the suit will be brought;

2. Give you some estimate as to how long the lawsuit will last; and

3. Make a determination of the approximate legal fees and disbursements.

If the lawyer sees weaknesses in your case and believes that litigation will be unduly expensive, he may advise you to compromise and settle the claim without resort to litigation. In any event, the chosen course of action should be instituted without delay so that you will be able to receive remuneration as quickly as possible. This will also ensure that the requisite time period to start the action, that is, the Statute of Limitations, will not have expired.

B. THE FEE ARRANGEMENT

Fees are derived after considering how much money you may recover from your lawsuit, the lawyer's expertise in handling this type of matter, and the degree of difficulty with the problem involved. The amount of time and effort to be spent on your behalf will also be considered when arriving at a suitable fee.

Your lawyer can usually estimate what the minimum and maximum limits of the fee will be. If such a figure seems high, do not hesitate to question the lawyer about it. If you feel that his explanation is inadequate, do not hesitate to tell him so. If necessary, inform him that you intend to speak with other lawyers about fees.

The fee arrangement is comprised of several elements which must be clearly understood. For example, costs are expenses that the attorney incurs while preparing your case. These include photocopying, telephone, mailing expenses, fees paid to the court for filing documents, and numerous other expenses. Be certain that the fee arrangement specifically mentions *in writing* which of these costs you must pay.

Different forms of fee arrangements are used by attorneys. These are:

1. Flat Fee

You may pay the lawyer one sum of money for the entire case. This may or may not include costs. Or both parties may find a flat-fee-plus-time-over arrangement more suitable. Here, a sum for a specified number of hours will be charged, and once the attorney works more hours than the specified number you will be charged on an hourly basis.

2. Hourly Rate

Many lawyers set their fees on an hourly basis computation. This hourly fee can range from $50 to $150 or more. Under this arrangement you will be charged a fixed hourly rate for all work done. If so, inquire whether phone calls are taken into account when determining the number of hours worked.

3. Contingency Fee

With this arrangement your attorney recovers a specified percentage of money if the case is successful. This usually ranges from 25 to 40 percent. Salesmen like this payment schedule because they are not required to pay an attorney his fee if their case is unsuccessful. However, ask your lawyer whether or not you are responsible for *costs* regardless of the outcome of your lawsuit. Have the terms of the contingency fee arrangement specified in writing

Helpful Hints

Regardless of the type of fee arrangement, you should bring a sum of money with you at the initial interview. This is called a retainer. It is an advance paid by you to demonstrate your desire to resolve your problem via legal recourse.

Inquire whether this payment is to become part of the entire fee and whether or not it is refundable.

When you call to make your initial appointment with the attorney, find out if you will be charged for the interview. Make sure that you are informed of the amount and basis for computing fees. The fee arrangement should always be in writing and signed by both parties to avoid misunderstandings.

In addition, ask that all fees be billed *periodically*. Insist that billing statements for services be supported by detailed and complete time records which include the number of hours worked and a description of the services rendered. Ask your attorney to send you copies of all incoming and outgoing correspondence so that you will be aware of the progress of your case.

Salesmen are reminded that they can shop around before selecting an attorney and may even change lawyers in the middle of their lawsuit. In the event you pay an attorney the interview fee and do not ultimately retain him, you are still ahead of the game provided you received a sound evaluation about the chances of success with your case.

7

PROTECTING THE SALESMAN FROM EXPLOITATION

SECTION 18
JOB MISREPRESENTATION

A. WHAT IS JOB MISREPRESENTATION?

Salesmen often respond to promising advertisements for employment which ask them to join organizations offering an unlimited potential for commission earnings. Such ads frequently state that the company uses national advertising to help sell the product for the salesman and that a dedicated staff will assist him in special sales and promotional matters. The salesman is then urged to join the ranks of company men who have already earned several million dollars even though they are not "high-pressure salesmen."

At his own expense the salesman then travels to the company's headquarters to inquire about the job. After the interview, he is told that he has been hired but must buy $5,000 worth of the product in order to sell it. Most salesmen decline the employment offer at this point. However, some accept and eventually discover that there is no organized sales force, nor is there a trained staff to assist the salesman with his selling duties.

The Federal Trade Commission protects salesmen from employment schemes such as these. Advertising designed to sell a product cannot be disguised as an employment offer. When the company states that you will earn a certain sum per year, this is deceptive if the figure is in excess of the average net earnings that its salesmen actually receive. Also, the Federal Trade Commission requires that:

1. If earnings are represented as "guaranteed," full disclosure must be made as to exactly what is offered by way of security;

2. The cooperation and assistance that salesmen will supposedly receive from their company cannot be misrepresented; and

3. Exclusive sales territories cannot be promised if they will not be allotted.

B. WHAT TO DO IF YOU ARE EXPLOITED

If you have been exploited, you should immediately file a complaint with the Federal Trade Commission. Direct all inquiries to: The Federal Trade Commission, Pennsylvania Avenue and Sixth Street, N.W., Washington, D.C. 20580.

The Federal Trade Commission has broad fact-finding powers. It can subpoena witnesses and documents relating to any matter under investigation and can impose fines and imprisonment if a company fails to supply requested evidence.

Once the Federal Trade Commission investigates alleged mistreatment, the agency may place a *cease and desist* order on the company. This prohibits the company from continuing misleading advertising and unfair employment practices. Such an investigation will have a deterrent effect and employers are generally afraid of dealing with the FTC. Thus, if you have been misled, you should "suggest" to your employer that you intend to file a complaint with the Federal Trade Commission. By doing so you will increase the likelihood of recovering expenses and extra commissions by means of a settlement.

Although money damages are generally not awarded under the Federal Trade Commissions Act, you may be able to recover money damages for false advertising practices under antitrust laws such as the Sherman and Clayton acts. In addition, if a salesmen is deceived by false advertising, he may seek a remedy via a claim for *fraud.* The salesman would have to prove that the company misrepresented facts that they knew were false but that were stated to induce the salesman to begin working for the company. If the salesman did not know that the statements were false, joined the company, and suffered economically, damages could be recovered.

Some state laws also grant remedies for victims of misleading trade practices and deceptive advertising. Statutes such as the Uniform Deceptive Trade Practices Act may have been passed in your state. These allow a salesman to sue for damages and equitable relief in addition to providing for action by the Attorney General. Thus, consult with an attorney before filing any claim in order to determine whether state laws are applicable.

Helpful Hints

To ensure that a future employer is not misleading you, ask him to authenticate his commission claims. Request that he show you the financial statements of the company's other salesmen. Have him remove their names if he claims that this information is confidential. In addition, ask for a written memorandum that states what your guaranteed minimum commission rate will be and the facts upon which such claims are based. If he is unwilling to do so after giving you the "hard sell," think twice before you begin spending valuable time and effort to sell his product.

Note: The Federal Trade Commission has ruled that the payment of a secret rebate by a customer to a salesman is an unfair practice. Salesmen cannot receive "push money" (rewards) from the sale of company goods without the consent of their employers.

SECTION 19
PROTECTING YOUR MONEY-MAKING IDEAS

Salesmen are frequently asked by their company to suggest ways in which business can be improved or become more efficient. Many times they voluntarily provide such information. While the policy of certain companies is to give bonuses for valuable suggestions, others simply use the idea without rewarding their salesmen. This section will briefly discuss the ways salesmen can protect themselves from such exploitation.

Consider the following situation: Richard, an independent selling agent, has a money-making plan and he tells his boss about it. His boss tells Richard that he likes it and that he "will be taken care of if the idea works out." The idea is subsequently used and it saves the company several thousand dollars. Richard does not receive a cent. Several months later, his contract is terminated. He sues to recover a percentage of the money that the company derived from his idea.

Richard does not have as strong a case as it may appear. According to the Federal Copyright Act of 1976, ideas, plans, methods, and procedures for business operations *cannot* be copyrighted. This means that even if the idea has been reduced to writing, no recovery can be obtained for voluntarily giving information to another.

However, various states have laws which afford protection to people such as Richard. Under the laws of several states, an idea will be protected if a court determines it to be a property interest. To qualify as such, the idea must be innovative, written in specific, concrete form, and rendered with the expectation of financial gain or a promotion. If all of these elements are proved, a state court may award damages, particularly if a salesman is subsequently discharged from his employment after his idea produces a substantial profit.

For protection, always consult with an attorney before giving your employer or any other person the use of an idea. Be certain that the idea or method is adequately described in writing. Have the person sign a document stating that if your idea is used, just compensaton will be given for it. The acknowledgment should include the following:

> *I, (Company), have received an idea from (Salesman). This idea is sufficiently original to me and it concerns _____.* If in the event the idea is used by the Company, its originator, (Salesman), will be compensated in good faith for its use. This idea will be carefully protected and shall not be disclosed to anyone without the prior written permission from (Salesman).*

SECTION 20
INCONVENIENCES WHILE "ON THE ROAD"

This section will discuss problems that salesmen encounter when traveling "on the road" and will reveal how you can receive compensation if you are inconvenienced.

A. PARKING LOT LIABILITY

Each year, thousands of salesmen have their cars stolen or broken into while parked in a lot. Although many salesmen have insurance to protect them from such incidents, it may also be possible to recover losses directly from the owner of the parking lot.

1. Parking Arrangements at the Lot

There are two different types of parking arrangements. In the first type an *attendant* takes control of your car at the entrance, gives you a claim check, places a duplicate of the check on the windshield, parks the car, and retains the keys. This creates a legal relationship known as a bailment.

In the second type of arrangement the *salesman* usually

---

*The idea can be for a variety of things. For example, it could be an advertising slogan, a new marketing technique, or an equipment innovation.

receives a claim check at the entrance, parks his car, locks it if he desires, retains the keys, and gives back the claim check when he pays the cashier at the lot exit. This is considered to be a leasing arrangement—you are leasing the parking space.

2. Liability If Your Car Is Stolen

If you park in a lot and leave your keys with an attendant, you can generally recover from the parking lot owner if your car is stolen.

If you park your car and retain the keys, the parking lot owner is usually *not* responsible if the car is stolen. However, the lot owner *will* be responsible if he or his attendants are negligent. For instance, if an attendant sees someone breaking into your car and fails to call the police, the lot owner will be responsible for the theft.

Even if you retain the keys, a number of states allow you to recover if the car is stolen from an enclosed lot. In one recent case a salesman parked and locked his car in an airport lot which was enclosed by a seven-foot fence. The lot contained a single means of entering and leaving. The court ruled that the owner of the lot was responsible when the salesman's car was stolen.

However, in another case in a different state, a salesman parked his car at an airport garage and entered by means of an automatic entrance gate which opened when a ticket was taken from the automatic dispenser. Here, the lot owner was *not* responsible when the car was subsequently stolen.

Whether the lot owner is responsible depends upon the law in your particular state. If you park the car, keep the keys, and your car is stolen, consult an attorney to determine if the lot owner is responsible. If an *attendant* parked your car, kept the keys, and the car is stolen, the lot owner is almost always responsible.

Note: If you leave your car in a parking lot *after* the lot has officially closed and are told in advance about closing time, you may not be able to recover if your car is stolen or broken into after hours.

3. Liability If Your Car Is Broken Into

If an *attendant* parks your car and keeps the keys, the parking lot owner will *not* be responsible if your car is broken into unless:

a. You *specifically* told an attendant that there were valuable goods in the car; and

b. The valuable goods in your car were plainly noticeable to anyone passing by your car.

For instance, Jane gave the car keys of her station wagon to an attendant who subsequently left the car unlocked. Six sample cases were in the back of the station wagon in plain view. She recovered the value of them when they were stolen.

Bernie, however, was not so fortunate. He had valuable sample cases in his trunk and intentionally did not disclose this to the attendant because he was afraid they would be stolen. When Bernie returned to his car, the cases were gone. He could not recover his loss because he did not inform the attendants about the samples. Thus, if you have valuable goods in your car and you give your keys to an attendant, inform him about the goods. You will then be able to recover their value if they are stolen.

In most instances, if you park the car and keep the keys, you will be unable to recover for your loss if your car is broken into.

4. Damages

If the parking lot attendant was aware of the contents in your car and your car is either stolen or broken into, you can recover all of the following expenses:

a. The total loss of the contents;

b. The cost of cab and airfare to obtain your clothes, personal effects, and additional samples;

c. The cost of renting a car;

d. The cost of sending someone to retrieve the car if found; and

e. Possible loss of earnings.

5. Disclaimers by the Parking Lot Owner

Parking lot owners frequently print disclaimers on ticket stubs which you receive. These state that the lot owner will not be responsible if your car is stolen or broken into. An example of a disclaimer follows:

> *This ticket entitles the lessee to the use of one parking space between the hours of 8:00 A.M. and 6:00 P.M. on the day issued. Lessor will endeavor to protect the property of the lessee but will not be responsible for loss or damage to cars, articles left therein, or accessories by reason of theft, accident, fire, or otherwise.*

Despite these disclaimers, lot owners are usually liable, and many states refuse to enforce them. A salesman's best defense is that he did *not* read the disclaimer. Courts will generally not enforce unread disclaimers, and he will be able to recover for his losses. However, be aware that a small number of states, including California, enforce certain disclaimers.

Lot owners frequently post signs that state that they will not be responsible for theft. These are not usually enforced by the courts. Again, your best defense is that you did *not* read the sign.

B. GETTING "BUMPED" BY THE AIRLINES

More than 150,000 people get bumped from the airlines each year. This occurs because airlines deliberately overbook; that is, they confirm reserved spaces for more passengers than can be carried on the flight.

When a greater number of reservation holders arrive for their desired flight than the airlines anticipated, the airlines will deny boarding to some of the ticket holders despite their reservations. This is referred to as "bumping."

Before bumping any passenger against his will, the airlines are required to request volunteers to relinquish their reservations in return for a payment of compensation. The volunteers are then paid a specified amount of money.

If you do *not* volunteer and are bumped, you are entitled to even *greater* compensation. The airline must furnish you with a written statement explaining how denied boarding compensation works. You are then entitled to receive the *face value* of your full one-way ticket. However, to obtain any compensation your ticket must have a minimum value of $37.50 and you cannot receive more than $200. If the airline cannot get you to your destination within two hours of the originally planned arrival time (four hours for an international flight), you will then be entitled to *twice* the value of your full one-way ticket ($75 minimum, $400 maximum).

Airlines *must* give you a check or money draft for this amount at the place and day when the bumping occurs. If you are placed on alternate transportation, you must be paid within twenty-four hours. Once you accept this compensation, the amount will serve as liquidated damages and is the *full* amount you can recover. You may refuse to accept this amount and sue the airline for damages.

Even if you are bumped, you will not be entitled to a refund if:

1. You fail to comply with the airline's ticketing, check-in, and reconfirmation requirements;

2. There is a government requisition of seats;

3. Safety or operational reasons prevent the flight; or

4. You are offered seating in a different section of the airplane.

C. GETTING "BUMPED" BY HOTELS

Salesmen are bumped from hotels in much the same manner as they are bumped from airlines. The hotels overbook to protect themselves from cancellations. If the hotel does not have a room available, you are entitled to get your deposit money back.

In most states a "confirmed hotel reservation" guarantees you *nothing* and you can only obtain your deposit if you sue. The following case is a typical example. Judy, an independent selling agent, confirmed a reservation and sent a check for $70 to the hotel. When she arrived there, she was told there were no rooms available. Judy was unable to obtain a room in any other hotel, so she returned to the airport and flew home. The court allowed Judy to recover her $70, since the hotel breached its contract, but she was not allowed to receive any money for loss of time from work, services, and/or travel expenses.

In a small number of states, if the hotel intentionally overbooks, it will be liable for special damages. You will be entitled to receive your deposit money back, damages for out-of-pocket losses, and money for emotional distress and disappointment. In one notable case a tourist recovered $600 when he was denied a room.

If you are bumped by a hotel because of overbooking, you may wish to file a claim in Small Claims Court. Unless the hotel has an agent or representative in your home state, you may have to file the lawsuit in the state where the hotel is located. Unfortunately, the expenses incurred in traveling to litigate the suit may make it impractical for you to sue the hotel.

Helpful Hints

If a local travel agent arranges your hotel reservations and you are bumped, you have a better chance of recovering damages if you sue the travel agent.

SECTION 21
THE COMPANY GOES BANKRUPT

Every year thousands of businesses file petitions in bankruptcy in the United States. This section will explain what a salesman should do to protect himself and how he can go about getting paid if his company goes bankrupt.

A. THE WARNING SIGNS OF BANKRUPTCY

In most cases the handwriting is on the wall before a business goes bankrupt. The decline of a business is usually a gradual process, and a salesman can protect himself well in advance of the bankruptcy if he knows what to look for.

The following symptoms are usually warning signs that a business is in trouble:

1. The Company Fails to Ship Goods

If the orders you are obtaining are not being filled by the company, this is a sign that the company is having financial difficulties. The company may be unable to obtain financing and cannot produce goods. Or the company may be having difficulty paying its bills to shippers. In any event, no company can survive unless its orders are shipped, since accounts receivable are the lifeline of the business.

2. The Company Fails to Pay Salary and/or Commissions

When companies are having financial difficulties, they frequently fall behind their payroll obligations. Salesmen are often told that the company is having "cash flow" problems which will be straightened out shortly. If the company's business is seasonal, this may be true. However, all too often "cash flow" problems are merely another way of saying that the company is going broke.

3. Creditors Fail to Get Paid

Many salesmen have contacts with customers who both buy and sell goods from their company. If you receive an abnormal number of complaints from customers who are owed money by your company, there may not be any money to pay them.

4. Comments Through the Grapevine

Your competitors or customers often hear rumors that your company is having financial problems. These rumors should not go unheeded, particularly if you notice the company is having problems paying its bills or shipping merchandise.

Note: If one of these warning signs is present, it does not mean that your company is going bankrupt. However, if all of these factors are present, it is time to start looking for another job. If you are concerned about the financial stability of your company, consider its track record. How long has the company been in existence? (Most businesses fail within their first few years.) Has the company had these types of problems in the past? Have you received a satisfactory explanation as to why the problems are occurring? Have key personnel recently left the company? The answers to these questions should help you decide if the company is in danger of going bankrupt.

B. THE COMPANY GOES BANKRUPT

A company can either voluntarily choose to declare bankruptcy or else it can be forced into bankruptcy by its creditors. The company will either be liquidated or reorganized. The bankruptcy proceeding begins when the company or the company's creditors file a document known as a petition with the bankruptcy court.

When a company is liquidated, its operations usually cease immediately or shortly after a petition has been filed with the bankruptcy court. The assets of the company are sold and creditors receive a pro rata share of the proceeds. This amount is frequently very small, that is, ten cents on the dollar.

Reorganization is a process by which a company is allowed to continue in operation yet still receive the benefits of having its debts discharged. A company proposes a plan to pay its creditors, that is, thirty cents on the dollar, which must be approved by the creditors. During a reorganization, the company will be run either by the same people or by a court-appointed trustee. If you continue working for the company during the reorganization, you are entitled to priority of payment for *all* salary and commissions that you earn. Payments to you are entitled to priority as an expense of administration.

C. FILING A CLAIM IN BANKRUPTCY

If your company goes bankrupt or is reorganized, it will be necessary for you to file a Proof of Claim to recover money you are owed. It is generally recognized that all salesmen, whether they be employees of the company or independent selling agents, are entitled to a priority claim for salary, commissions, and all other benefits (for example, vacation pay) earned within ninety days of the filing of the petition in bankruptcy up to $2,000.

Priority payments are paid in full before general trade creditors are paid. If there is sufficient money on hand, you will be paid up to $2,000. However, if you earn and are owed *over* $2,000 within ninety days of the time that the company goes bankrupt, you will only be entitled to a general unsecured claim for the money that is owed in excess of $2,000. For instance, Brad earns $3,000 in commissions ten days before his company goes bankrupt. He is entitled to file a claim for $3,000—a priority claim for $2,000 and a general unsecured claim for $1,000. Brad may be paid in full on the $2,000 claim yet only receive ten cents on the dollar for the $1,000 portion of his claim. Similarly, if Miles earns and is owed $5,000 in commissions one hundred days before the company goes bankrupt, he is only entitled to a general unsecured claim for $5,000 (that is, perhaps ten cents on the dollar).

If your company goes bankrupt and you are owed money, you will receive a notice from the court that states where to file a proof of claim. If you do not receive a notice, you should contact officials of the company, the company attorney, or other creditors to discover this information.

The following is an example of a proof of claim. For purposes of this illustration, assume that Debtor, Inc., goes bankrupt on July 1, 1981. John Doe, a company salesman, earned $5,000 in commissions within ninety days of the filing of the petition in bankruptcy:

UNITED STATES BANKRUPTCY COURT
FOR THE <u>CENTRAL</u> DISTRICT OF <u>CALIFORNIA</u>

In re
DEBTOR, INC.   Bankruptcy 81–1111
Debtor
*(include here all names used by bankrupt/debtor within
last 6 years)*

PROOF OF CLAIM FOR WAGES, SALARY, OR
COMMISSION

   1. The debtor owes the claimant $5,000.00 com-
puted as follows:

      (a) wages, salary, or commission for services
performed on April 1, 1981 to June 30, 1981, at
the following rate or rates of compensation (if
appropriate)

               $5,000.00

      (b) allowances and benefits, such as vacation
and severance pay (specify)

      _____

      _____

      Total amount claimed $5,000.00

   2. The claimant demands priority to the extent permitted by Section 507 (a) (5) of the Bankruptcy
Code. $2,000.00.
   3. The claimant has received no payment, no security, and no check or other evidence of the debt, except as follows . . . *(state whether you were paid
any money on this obligation, whether you retained
samples to offset the debt, etc.)*
Dated:

          Signed:_____JOHN DOE_____
                             Claimant
          Social Security Number_____
          Address:_____

   Penalty for Presenting Fraudulent Claim: Fine up to $5,000 or imprison-
onment for not more than five years or both.

Helpful Hints

1. If your company has not declared bankruptcy and you are owed money that is due greater than ninety days, have all payments you receive prior to the bankruptcy made specifically on account of your oldest salary and commission claims. For instance, if you had not been paid your weekly salary for five weeks and you then received a weekly pay check, have your company note on the check, or in a letter, that the check you received is for your salary that was due five weeks before and is not payment of your current weekly wages. This will allow you to claim a greater portion of the debt as priority.

2. Do *not* delay in filing your claim. If you fail to file a claim, you may not get paid.

3. Do *not* expect to receive payment quickly. It may take several years before your claim is processed and you are paid.

4. Take a "bad debt deduction" on your federal and state income taxes for any monies that you are not paid. It is wise to contact your tax consultant on matters pertaining to bad debt deductions.

5. Attach copies of all documents to support your claim.

8

TAX TIPS FOR THE SALESMAN

1. INTRODUCTION

For your convenience we have provided you with a detailed list of deductions that can be used to reduce your gross income and serve as a tremendous source of tax savings. Travel and entertainment expenses are usually examined closely by the Internal Revenue Service upon audit. Many individuals who are audited suffer a disallowance of legitimate expenses due to their failure to satisfy substantiation requirements. Thus, salesmen should be informed of these rules in order to protect themselves. If you consult an accountant regularly you are probably aware of some of the following rules and will find that this chapter is a good review. If you are not aware of these rules, we suggest that they be read with great care. Some of the following information was obtained directly from IRS publications.

2. TRAVEL EXPENSES

    a. Are the ordinary and necessary expenses incurred while traveling away from the "tax home," *overnight*, in pursuit of your business demands;

    b. Cannot be incurred for personal or vacation purposes;

    c. Cannot be lavish or extravagant;

    d. Must be substantiated by accurate, detailed records; and

e. Should not be confused with the smaller category of transportation expenses (see number 3 in this chapter).

In order to obtain travel expense deductions, a salesman must be away from his "tax home." The tax home is considered to be a salesman's:

a. Company headquarters if he returns there to conduct business at least several times a year;

b. Principal place of business if he regularly works for two or more companies (determined by the company where he spends the most time and earns the most money);

c. Home or apartment if he does not return to his company's headquarters; or

d. *No tax home* if he does not live in an established residence and does not return to his company's headquarters (example: he sends all of his orders to the company and receives his commission checks and statements by mail). If so, then he will be considered an itinerant and *cannot* claim a traveling expense deduction, since his residence happens to be the place where he works.

Helpful Hints

If you are an unmarried salesman who travels extensively and does not live in an established residence, it is wise to incur some expense and rent a room within your territory on a full-time basis in order to receive a traveling expense deduction for meals and lodging. You should maintain a mailing address to indicate proof of permanent residence.

a. The deductions

You may deduct all of the following expenses incurred after you leave your tax home that are business-related:

1. Air, rail, and bus fares;
2. Operation and maintenance of your automobile;
3. Taxi fares or other costs of transportation between the airport or station and your hotel, from one customer to another, or from one place of business to another;
4. Transportation from the place where you obtain your meals and lodging to your temporary work assignment;

5. Baggage charges and transportation costs for sample and display material;

6. Meals and lodging when you are away from home on business;

7. Cleaning and laundry expenses;

8. Telephone and telegraph expenses;

9. Public stenographers' fees;

10. Operation and maintenance of house trailers;

11. Tips that are incidental to any of these expenses; and

12. Similar expenses incident to qualifying travel.

There are certain limitations to this list. For example, travel expenses for meals and lodging incurred while on your business trip cannot be deducted unless you *actually sleep* and you must prove a release from the job in order to secure sleep. Pulling over to the side of a road and taking a two-hour nap will not suffice.

b. Record keeping

It is easy to plan for the deductibility of travel expenses if you follow the rules set forth in this section. Salesmen should keep careful, detailed accounts of all expenditures. The IRS requires strong proof of travel expenses; approximations are usually not acceptable in this area. Salespeople should substantiate all expenditures in an account book, diary, statement of expense, or similar record, and support these with corresponding documentation. For example, entries on a desk calendar not supported by evidence are not proper substantiation.

In order for your travel expenses to be deductible, you must be able to prove the following:

1. The *amount* of each expenditure for travel away from home, such as the cost of your transportation or lodging, but the daily cost of your breakfast, lunch, dinner, and other incidental elements of travel may be totaled if they are set forth in reasonable categories (that is, meals, gasoline and oil, and taxi fares);

2. The *dates* of your departure and return home for

each trip and the number of days spent on business away from home;

3. The *destination* of your travel described by city or town; and

4. The *business reason* and benefit expected to be gained by your travel.

Salesmen must save all receipts and keep their records timely in order to ensure that they receive maximum deductions for these expenses. It is a good idea to spend fifteen minutes every Monday morning collecting and reporting the travel and entertainment expenses of the past week.

Helpful Hints

IRS agents are advised to carefully scrutinize all expenses charged via credit cards. Thus, watch for the mixed use of credit cards. To avoid questions, use one or more credit cards *only* for business and the rest only for personal use.

A canceled check together with a bill from the vendor will ordinarily establish the element of cost. However, a canceled check will not by itself support a business expenditure without other evidence to show that the check was for a business purpose.

Two favorite areas of investigation by IRS agents involving traveling expenses concern airline tickets and lodging receipts.

Airline tickets will show:

a. The name of the passenger;

b. The name of the company or individual who purchased the ticket;

c. The method of payment–IRS agents are aware of reimbursements for expenses initially charged to a business account;

d. The date of the departure and return, since this will indicate whether the trip was extended beyond business days;

e. The destinations, since this may indicate stops made en route to or from the business destination; and

f. The cost—whether for coach, first class, or family plan.

Lodging receipts:

a. Will help establish if the travel is away from home overnight and whether the accommodations are for single or double occupancy; and

b. IRS agents are instructed to investigate third-party sources such as hotel directories and hotel reservation services to explain and identify items on lodging receipts.

Thus, travel in the coach section so that your travel expenses will not appear excessive and avoid excess lodging expenses.

c. Additional information

Deductions are allowed for ordinary and necessary travel expenses paid in connection with sales activities and reduced by reimbursements received as additional compensation and reported on the salesman's W-2 form. Deductions are allowed for unreimbursed travel expenses even if they are incurred beyond the salesman's assigned territory. Travel and related expenses are not allowed if they are incurred while searching for new employment or while investigating a new business.

d. Convention expenses

Meals, lodging, and all other expenses are deductible for convention expenses as long as your attendance advances the interests of your business. They are deductible even if attendance provides personal as well as business benefits. However, the convention must be business-related and cannot promote social or political causes.

IRS agents are instructed to carefully scrutinize convention and meeting agendas in order to determine the business relationship of the proceedings. They look at:

1. The nature of the business conducted;

2. The amount of time actually spent on business at the convention;

3. The social events included on the agenda; and

4. The site and time of the meeting to determine if the convention was vacation-oriented (example: a salesmen's convention held in Miami during the month of January). How-

ever, the fact that there are social events scheduled at a convention in a resort area does not mean that the convention expenses are not deductible.

Helpful Hints

You want to be able to prove that the convention attracted fellow salesmen with similar business interests and duties. Thus, save all convention pamphlet materials and agenda receipts. If possible, obtain a certificate that states that you attended the convention and have a convention official sign a document indicating that you were present and had an excellent attendance record throughout the meetings. Typically, convention officials provide "sign in" sheets for this purpose since the IRS often reviews these sheets.

e. Travel within the United States

Deductions are allowed for all travel expenses to and from a destination in the United States if the travel was primarily for business reasons. Since the amount of time spent on personal activities compared with the time spent for business is an important factor in determining whether the travel was primarily for pleasure, salesmen should try to establish a favorable time sequence. If you intend to engage in personal activities, you should do so after arriving at your destination on weekends.

f. Travel outside of the United States

Traveling to a destination other than Washington, D.C., and the fifty states is regarded as being outside of the United States. Elaborate rules have been established by the IRS concerning the deductibility of personal and business travel outside of the United States. If your travel was primarily for business but there were some nonbusiness activities, you may not be able to deduct all of your travel costs (especially meals to and from your business destination), and your expenses will probably be allocated between business and nonbusiness activities.

Helpful Hints

The IRS is extremely sensitive to travel outside the United States with personal overtones. To increase the chances of deducting all traveling expenses, the salesman should:

1. Avoid taking his spouse or other family members with him;

2. Make the business portion of the travel long when compared to the total period of absence; and

3. Be able to easily justify the business benefits that were derived from the trip.

g. Spouse expenses and traveling deductions

Usually, spouse deductions are not allowed unless the salesman can prove that his wife's presence was necessary to further his trade. On these trips she must perform more than the mere spousal functions of attending social functions and entertaining business acquaintances. However, if a wife qualifies for the deduction, a salesman can deduct expenses to conventions as well as her meal and lodging expenses.

Helpful Hints

A salesman has a stronger claim to this deduction if he shows that his wife actually sells to his customers on her own and that she sells even when they are not traveling. This can be documented by a letter from a customer stating that goods were sold to him by the salesman's spouse. The importance of the spouse's services may also be demonstrated by a showing that she is knowledgeable in the working affairs of the business. You should obtain a similar letter from your company as well.

3. TRANSPORTATION EXPENSES

Transportation expenses include the cost of operating and maintaining your automobile in addition to travel by air, bus, or train. If you work for two or more companies, trips from one company to the other on the same day are deductible as travel expenses. However, commuting expenses between your residence and principal place of business are not deductible.

a. Automobile expenses

Automobile expenses include:

1. Cost of gasoline and oil;
2. Repairs;
3. Insurance;

4. Depreciation;
5. Interest required to purchase the car; and
6. Taxes, licenses, garage rent, parking fees, and tolls.

b. Apportionment

If you use your car exclusively as a sales representative, you can deduct the entire cost of its operation. If you use your car for both personal and business purposes, you must apportion the expense. Simply divide your business mileage (this does not include mileage incurred when driving to and from your home) from the total number of miles you drive each year.

> Example: 30,000 business miles
> ‾‾‾‾‾‾‾‾‾‾‾‾‾‾‾‾‾‾‾‾
> 40,000 total miles

Using this formula, you can deduct 75 percent of your automobile expenses. If you lease your car, you may also deduct lease payments to the extent that they are attributable to your trade or business.

There are two ways to calculate your automobile expenses. Using the *itemized method*, you total up all actual operating and fixed expenses including depreciation of your car. Using the *standard method*, you receive a standard deduction of $.20 a mile for the first 15,000 business miles and $.11 for each additional business mile. You cannot use the standard method unless you own the car and use a normal straight line method for depreciation purposes. If your car had been fully depreciated, you can only obtain a maximum $.11 per mile deduction.

Helpful Hints

The itemized and standard methods can be changed from year to year. If you incur huge expenses for repairs but drive fewer miles than the year before, you are free to switch from the standard to the itemized method. In the following year you could then switch back to the standard method if this makes economic sense. Thus, choose the method that saves you the most money.

Salesmen cannot obtain deductions for fines from violations of traffic regulations or for the expenses given to a driver of a car pool. However, money received from the passengers of a car pool does not have to be included in gross income.

c. Record keeping

You must maintain adequate records to establish the actual business mileage of your car. Estimates are *not* acceptable. Thus, save all toll receipts. The amount of money spent on tolls will surprise you. IRS agents are instructed to carefully scrutinize all mileage claims, since these are often overstated. They refer to repair bills at the beginning and end of the year because these bills often contain a mileage reading. In addition, the agents allocate automobile expenses between business and personal use by referring to the automobile insurance policy. The policy will state whether other members of the family operate the vehicle. They also check signatures of credit cards for gas purchases and examine oil change and gas receipts. Additionally, IRS agents exclude travel to and from work from business mileage.

4. COMMUTING EXPENSES

1. Are expenses incurred by a salesman traveling between his residence and place of business, and are *not* deductible;

2. Are deductible once he arrives at his primary work location and then travels to a second job or location.

Be aware that if you transport samples or other products to your principal place of work and you incur additional costs because of these materials, you *can* deduct transportation expenses that exceed your normal commuting costs. For example, if you usually take the train to work but must rent a car in order to return your sample line, you can deduct the difference between the car rental and the train fare. However, you must be able to *prove* what these additional expenses are.

5. BUSINESS GIFTS

If a salesman makes a gift to an individual and the gift is ordinary, necessary, and incurred in connection with his trade or business, he may deduct up to $25 a year for each person to whom he gave such gifts. Examples of gifts include jewelry, packaged food, and beverages to be consumed at a later date. Gifts to the wife of a business customer are treated as though they were given to the customer himself, unless the wife has a bona fide connection with the salesman separate from her husband. For example, David is a retail salesman of women's apparel who deals with Jeff and Cindy. They are married and own a small boutique. Jeff does the buying and Cindy runs the daily activities of the shop. If David makes $25 gifts to both of them, he will probably be able to obtain a total deduction of $50.

Exceptions to the $25 rule

A salesman is entitled to unlimited deductions greater than $25 for:

a. Items costing $4 or less on which the salesman's name is clearly and permanently imprinted and is one of a number of identical items distributed by the salesman. This includes pens, desk sets, plastic bags and cases;

b. Advertising signs, display racks, and other promotional material to be used on the business premises of the recipient; and

c. Incidental costs such as engraving jewelry, packaging, or mailing.

Incidental costs are *not* usually included when applying the $25 limit. A related cost is not incidental if it adds substantially to the value of the gift. For example, if you buy $25 worth of fruit for a customer and then purchase a $15 basket for the fruit, the cost of the basket will not be deductible.

Record keeping

The following elements must be proved for business gifts:

a. The cost of the gift;
b. When it was made;
c. A description of the gift;
d. The reason for making the gift or the business benefit expected to be gained; and

e. The occupation and other information about the person to whom you gave the gift to establish a sufficient business relationship.

Tax tips

Business gifts may be timed to work within the $25 limitation. If you wish, for example, to give a customer four bottles of wine (cost of $12.50 each) as a Christmas gift, you should transfer two bottles ($25 value) to him in December, and an additional two bottles ($25 value) in early January of the following new year.

Salesmen should recognize that if they have a choice between classification of a business gift or business entertainment they should use the more favorable classification. For example, tickets to a theater or sporting event can be treated as either an entertainment expense or a gift.

Although business gifts are limited to $25 per person per year, business entertainment expenses have no set limit. If you accompany the customer to the sporting event or theater, the cost of the tickets will be treated as an entertainment expense and not a gift. However, the salesman must prove that a bona fide business discussion took place either preceding or following the event.

6. ENTERTAINMENT EXPENSES

In general, entertainment expenses are deductible if you can show that:

a. You engaged in business with the person being entertained;

b. The main purpose of the combined business and entertainment was the transaction of business; and

c. You had more than a general expectation of deriving income or benefit at some time in the future.

In order to qualify for the deduction, you do not have to prove that a benefit actually resulted from the expenditure. Nor do you have to prove that more time was devoted to business than to entertainment. In addition, expenses incurred for the creation or maintenance of business *goodwill are* deductible.

a. Record keeping

To receive the deduction, you must maintain accurate records that prove:

1. The amount of each separate expenditure for entertaining (except for incidental items, such as taxi fares and telephone calls, which may be totaled on a daily basis);

2. The date the entertainment took place;

3. The name, address or location, and the type of entertainment, such as dinner or theater;

4. The reason for the entertainment or the business benefit derived or expected to be gained from entertaining and the nature of any business discussion or activity that took place; and

5. The occupation and other information about the persons entertained. This should include the name, title, or other designation sufficient to establish the business relationship with you.

In terms of issues considered by an IRS agent upon audit, entertainment expenses usually head the list. This is because salesmen often claim business expenses for nondeductible personal living expenses.

Salesmen must remember that their entertainment expenses cannot be lavish. However, an entertainment expense will not be considered lavish merely because it involves first-class accommodations or services, and IRS agents examine the facts of each case before reaching a conclusion.

b. Restaurants and nightclubs

Expenses incurred at restaurants and nightclubs are deductible if you can show that a meal was furnished to an individual in an atmosphere generally conducive to business discussions. Generally, a nightclub or place where entertainment is a major attraction is not considered to be a suitable environment for a business discussion.

You may be able to deduct the cost of a meal the preceding evening if a business discussion is held the following day. For example, Phyllis and her husband entertain several out-of-town customers at a local restaurant on a Friday evening. No business is discussed. The next morning at breakfast, she spends time discussing the products that her company sells. If the business "pitch" at breakfast can be proved, she may be able to deduct the expenses of both meals. Her husband's meal can also be deducted provided she demonstrates a clear business purpose.

IRS agents are instructed to review your meal checks. These must disclose the date, name, and location of the place where the entertainment occurred in addition to the amount of the meal. The agents look at the number of persons served and are particularly alert in attempting to discover whether the dining was a *reciprocal arrangement* with social rather than business overtones.

c. Home parties

If you entertain at home, purchases of food and liquor are deductible. You may gain the deduction if the entertaining is done for goodwill business purposes. However, IRS agents will carefully scrutinize your records to ascertain the purpose of these parties. Weddings, birthdays, and anniversary parties are not deductible.

You should save all guest lists to correlate the amount of purchases with the number of guests at the party. If you frequently entertain at your home, purchase your food and liquor at a different store from the place where you normally buy such items. If you save all receipts from this store, you will be able to prove that all purchases from X Liquor Store and Y Food Store were solely for business.

d. Entertainment facilities

Entertainment facilities include yachts, hunting lodges, fishing camps, swimming pools, tennis courts, airplanes, etc. The expenses attributable to the use of the facility include depreciation and general operating costs such as rent, utility charges, insurance, and repairs. All of the above were once potential business expense deductible items. However, the IRS has now ruled that you cannot deduct amounts paid or incurred for any entertainment facility *except a country club.*

With regard to country clubs, which include golf clubs, social and sports clubs, IRS agents are instructed to:

a. Examine the monthly statements of expenses from the files of the facility as well as from the salesman;

b. Analyze the signatures on the charges to determine if individuals other than the salesman used the facility;

c. Examine the types of items purchased and the activities engaged in; and

d. Be alert for the possible inclusion of personal expenses such as clothing, golf equipment, accessories, and tennis lessons.

Helpful Hint

One permissible method to determine that the primary use of the facility is for business is to establish that more than 50 percent of the total calendar days of use are for business purposes. If you go to the club for a business-related lunch, the entire meal is deductible even if you cannot deduct the club dues.

7. BUSINESS USE OF YOUR HOME

The business part of your home:

a. Is that part of your home that is *solely* used for business and not personal use;

b. Must be located in your residence or garage and not in a hotel, motel or similar establishment;

c. Must be used on a continuing basis for you to meet with your customers or store your lines, products, and inventory that are used in your business.

If you have met these tests, divide the area allocated for business purposes by the entire area of your home. For example:

<u>500 sq. ft.</u> of business space
10,000 sq. ft. of total living space in your home

If you arrive at a 5 percent figure, you may deduct 5 percent of the expenses directly related to the business portion of your home. These include depreciation, rent, utilities, and insurance. You may also deduct *in full*, direct expenses made to that area (such as painting and repairs).

Thus, keep detailed records of all expenditures attributable to business use for maintaining your home in order to obtain this deduction.

8. MOVING EXPENSE DEDUCTIONS

Your moving expenses are deductible providing you meet the following requirements:

a. The new place of work must be at least thirty-five miles farther than your old residence was from your former place of work;

b. Independent selling agents must work full-time for at least thirty-nine weeks of the twelve-month period following the move; and

c. The move must have been in connection with the start of work at the new location.

To be deductible, all moving expenses must be reasonable. Presently, you are allowed a maximum deduction of $3,000 for all expenses. However, no more than $1,500 may be deducted for house-hunting trips and temporary quarters. The other deductible items include:

a. Real estate commissions, attorney's fees, title and escrow fees;

b. Loan placement charges; and

c. State transfer taxes.

The above items may be deducted when you sell your former home and buy a new residence. However, you may not deduct the cost of physical improvements intended to enhance the salability of your old residence.

Conclusion

Congratulations. Now that you have read this book carefully, you have increased your knowledge of contract law and have acquired a better understanding of your legal rights. Hopefully, this knowledge will be used to protect your interests and further your careers.

Although this book cannot replace a lawyer, it will steer you in the proper direction to solve your problems. The book should be kept in some prominent place for easy reference, and portions should be reread whenever problems arise in your daily business dealings. If you encounter a minor problem, you now have the means to resolve it by meeting with an authorized representative of your company or else instituting suit in Small Claims Court. If you believe that a significant amount of money is involved, you should not be penny-wise and pound-foolish—obtain the services of an attorney who is experienced in handling employment contract disputes and salesman's law.

When you are negotiating your employment agreement, remember that there is no limit to the types of provisions that can be contained within it. Imaginative use of your contract can result in significant tax savings besides enhanced job security. In addition, the best protection is always a written contract that clearly defines the terms and conditions of employment. This forces both parties to seriously think about their working relationship. Many salespeople are afraid to ask for terms that a reasonable business person would request because they are anxious to obtain a product to sell and fear that if they make too many demands the company will withdraw its offer of employment. Unfortunately, this often occurs. However, salespeople who are about to agree to represent a company and expend their best effort and money to sell a product must discuss important terms forthrightly with potential employers before they begin working. A salesman should receive written assurance that the company will promptly pay commissions and furnish invoice copies of all merchandise shipped into the salesman's territory, ship qualified accounts within a reasonable time, and generally exercise good faith. If the company is reluctant to do any of these things, you may be better off finding someone or something else to represent.

All salespeople should apply the principles of preventative "medicine" to their business activities. For example, an arrangement should be made whereby you will receive commissions and commission statements on a biweekly or monthly basis. This payment schedule makes it easier to keep track of earned commissions and significantly reduces the possibility of forfeiting these commissions in the event that your services are terminated. If you maintain careful records of your business transactions, send letters that document your agreements, and avoid oral promises, you will maximize your claims in the event that an employer breaches your contract. This information will enhance your legal position whether you decide to settle a dispute or litigate the problem in court.

The rest is up to you. Using this book as your guide, and with an attorney to advise you about applicable laws in your state, you will minimize potential areas of conflict and enjoy a financially satisfying and pleasant working relationship.

Glossary of Terms

The terms included in this section are frequently used in legal proceedings, and salespeople should be aware of their meanings.

Accord and satisfaction An agreement by the salesman and his company to compromise disputes concerning outstanding debts, compensation, or employment terms. Satisfaction occurs when the salesman and company perform the terms of the compromise.

Affidavit A written statement signed under oath.

Allegations Written statements in pleadings by parties in a lawsuit that explain what the parties expect to prove in the case.

Answer The defendant's reply to the plaintiff's complaint. It is usually the second document filed in the lawsuit. In the answer the defendant may deny many and possibly all of the allegations contained in the plaintiff's complaint by stating, for example, that they are untrue.

Anticipatory breach A breach of contract that occurs when one party, i.e., the salesman, states in advance of performance that he will definitely not perform under the terms of his contract.

Arbitration A hearing similar to a court trial except that the case is decided by arbitrators rather than a judge and no jury is present.

Breach of contract The unjustified failure of a party to a contract, i.e., the salesman or company, to perform a duty or obligation under the terms of the contract.

Cause of action A claim or claims the plaintiff asserts in his complaint that sets forth the legal theories upon which the lawsuit is based.

Clerk of the court The person usually responsible for overseeing that all court documents are properly filed. In a Small Claims Court proceeding the clerk will issue summonses, and answer your questions concerning procedures and calendar dates.

Compensatory damages A sum of money awarded to the salesman or company that is equal to the amount of actual losses suffered as a result of a breach of contract.

Complaint The first pleading filed by the plaintiff which begins a lawsuit. The complaint states the facts and legal theories of the plaintiff's case.

Consideration Something of value given or promised by the salesman/company including services, money, or property in exchange for an act or promise by the company/salesman. Consideration is necessary to make a contract enforceable.

Continuance A postponement of a scheduled court hearing to a later date.

Contract An oral or written agreement that sets forth the salesman's employment terms; for example, his commission rate, territory, and duties.

Covenant A promise, either contained in a contract or agreed upon after the contract has been entered into.

Damages A sum of money awarded to the salesman/company as compensation for losses or injuries resulting from a breach of contract or negligence by the other party.

Default judgment A judgment awarded to the plaintiff/defendant if the defendant/plaintiff does not appear at the court trial.

Defendant A person or company sued in a lawsuit.

Deposition A proceeding where oral testimony of one of the parties or witnesses in a lawsuit is taken before the trial. An attorney will question the opposing party, usually in an attorney's office, and the statements of the party or witness are taken under oath by a court stenographer.

Duress Unlawful threats or conduct that compel a salesman/company to enter, disavow, or perform a contract. The person who is threatened is not bound by the contract.

Evidence Includes oral testimony of witnesses, documents, and exhibits that properly give information to a court in order to establish matters of fact.

Fraud   Intentional false statements or conduct regarding an important existing fact that is relied upon, causing harm to the defrauded party.

Guaranty   A contract where one person agrees to answer for or satisfy the debt of another upon that person's default.

Implied in fact contract   A contract found to exist as a result of the working relationship between parties rather than by an expressly agreed upon oral or written contract.

Impossibility of performance   Circumstances that make it impossible for a party to perform the terms of a contract and thus excuse him from responsibility for damages caused by a breach of contract. These events will usually be unforeseeable if they are to serve as a valid legal excuse for nonperformance.

Injunction   An order of the court that prohibits a person/company from doing or refusing to do a particular act.

Interrogatories   A series of written questions sent to an opponent designed to discover information prior to trial. The opponent must then reply, under oath, with written answers to these questions usually within thirty days.

Liquidated damages   An amount of money agreed upon in advance by the parties to a contract that is to be paid as damages if a party breaches the contract.

Mitigation of damages   A requirement that a party who claims damages must make reasonable efforts to reduce damages as much as possible; for example, to look for a new job after being terminated.

Nominal damages   A small sum of money (perhaps $1.00) awarded by the court for damages resulting from a breach of contract.

Offer   A specific proposal by one person to another that is either oral or written and results in a contract when it is accepted.

Party   A plaintiff or defendant in a lawsuit.

Perjury   Intentional false testimony by a party or witness concerning an important fact at a court hearing or other matter where the party or witness has taken an oath.

Plaintiff   A person who initiates the lawsuit.

Pleadings   Written allegations by parties to a lawsuit that set forth their legal claims and defenses.

Power of attorney   A signed document that authorizes a person to perform certain acts on your behalf as your agent or attorney.

Pretrial discovery   Various procedures used before trial to obtain facts, documents, and other records of your opponent to be used as evidence on your behalf. Interrogatories, depositions, and Notice to Produce Documents are examples of pretrial discovery devices.

Punitive damages   Monetary damages assessed as punishment for a party's reckless and malicious acts. Also referred to as exemplary damages.

Rescission   The cancellation of a contract resulting in the restoration of both parties to their original position prior to the time they entered into the contract.

Specific performance   A court order that requires a party to perform under the terms of his contract rather than pay damages.

Statute of frauds   A rule of law providing that employment contracts are not enforceable if for a term in excess of one year unless the contract is in writing and signed by the party who has allegedly breached the contract.

Statute of limitations   A law stating the requisite time period within which a lawsuit must be brought. Failure to bring suit within this time precludes you from obtaining an award by the court.

Subpoena   A court order requiring a witness to appear at court to testify.

Summons   A certified document issued by the court that informs the person whose name appears on it that a lawsuit has begun against him, that he must answer the complaint, and that he must appear in court on a specified date.

Void   Legally unenforceable.

Waiver   A voluntary and intentional surrender of a known right.

Index

A

Accord and Satisfaction, 76–79
    definition, 76–77
    of disputed debts, 78–79
    of undisputed debts, 77–78
Airline bumping, 101–103
    denied boarding
        compensation, 102
    overbooking, 101
Arbitration, 79–84
    advantages of, 81
    by contractual provision,
        80–81
    disadvantages of, 81–84
    removal to, 84
    submission agreements,
        79–80

B

Bankruptcy, 103–108
    filing procedures, 106–108
    petition, 105, 107
    proof of claim, 105–108
    reorganization, 105
Breach of Contract, 62–71
    compensatory damages, 63

definition of, 62
liquidated damages, 63,
    69–71
nominal damages, 63

C

Commissions, 18–35, 68
    advances, 32–35
    alteration of rate, 28–29
    definition of, 18
    earned by accepted orders,
        18–19
    earned by shipped orders,
        19–21
    eighty-five percent
        guarantee, 20–21, 83
    guarantees, 29–32
    impossibility of
        performance, 21–22
    key account salesmen, 24
    lump sum payments, 25, 125
    off-price goods, 22–23, 42
    reorders, 25–26
    residuals, 29
    voluntary resignations,
        23–24

D

Duties of Salespeople:
  exceeding authority, 43
  generally, 43–46
  loyalty, 43, 68–69
  making secret profits, 44–45,
    96
  mitigation of damages,
    65–66
  revealing trade secrets,
    45–46
  working for a competitor, 44,
    76

F

Federal Trade Commission, 37,
    95–96
  Clayton Act, 37, 96
  Federal Trade Commissions
    Act, 96
  fraud remedies, 96
  Uniform Deceptive Trade
    Practices Act, 96

H

Hiring your lawyer, 90–93
  costs, 91–92
  fees generally, 91–93
    contingency fee, 92
    flat fee, 92
    hourly fee, 92
  initial interview, 90
  retainer, 92
Hotel bumping, 102–103
  confirmed hotel reservations,
    102
  damages, 103
  deposits, 102–103

I

Independent Selling Agents,
    15–17, 48
  status of, 16–17
  versus employee status, 17
Inspection and Discovery, 75,
    82–83

J

Job misrepresentation, 94–96

M

Modifications, 51–56
  by contract, 52–53
  most favored party clause,
    55–56
  oral modifications, 53–56
  Parol Evidence Rule, 54
Money-Making Ideas, 97–98
  Federal Copyright Act of
    1976, 97

O

Oral contracts, 2–6, 32, 34
  hired by telephone, 5–6
  Statute of Frauds, 4

P

Parking lot liability, 98–101
  bailments, 98
  damages, 100
  disclaimers, 101
Proper Accounting, 8, 39–42
  commission statements, 42
  computer errors, 41
  discovery, 41
  provisions for, 39–41

R

Rescission, 56–61
  by contract, 58–60
  by court decree, 61
  by fraud, duress, or mistake,
    54, 57, 60–61
  by mutual consent, 57–58
  definition of, 56–57
Restrictive Covenants, 45–50,
  69
  damages, 50
  definition of, 46
  injunctive relief, 50

S

Sidelines, 44, 76
Small Claims Court, 39, 73,
  84–90, 91, 124
  amount of money, 85–86
  duties of salespeople, 88
  filing for, 86–87
  obtaining judgement, 89–90
  the trial, 89
Statute of Limitations, 91

T

Tax tips, 109–23
  business gifts, 117–19
  commuting expenses, 117
  convention expenses, 113,
    115
  credit cards, 112
  entertainment expenses,
    119–22

facilities, 121–22
    parties, 121
    restaurants and nightclubs,
      120–21
  home use, 122
  moving expenses, 123
  spouse deductions, 115
  transportation expenses,
    115–17
  travel expenses, 109–15
Termination of Contracts,
    8–13, 26–27, 64–65, 67
  corrective action, 11
  good cause, 12–13
  notice of, 9–11
Territorial Rights, 8, 35–38, 68
  commissions, 36–38
  exclusive selling agent,
    35–37
  house accounts, 37–38, 42
  out of territory accounts, 38

U

Unjust Enrichment, 71–73
  quantum meruit, 71

W

Waiver, 68
Written contracts, 7–15
  definite term, 13, 64, 67
  employment at will, 7–9, 64,
    67
  lifetime contracts, 14–15

About the Authors

STEVEN MITCHELL SACK

Steven Mitchell Sack is a Phi Beta Kappa graduate of Stony Brook University and Boston College Law School. He practices law in New York City and is legal counsel for SESAC INC.

Mr. Sack enjoys lecturing and writing articles which provide the public with helpful legal solutions to their most pressing problems. He has served as a guest speaker for various organizations including the Bureau of Wholesale Sales Representatives and the Conference of Personnel Managers.

HOWARD JAY STEINBERG

Howard Jay Steinberg is an attorney practicing in Los Angeles, California. He is associated with the law firm of Gendel, Raskoff, Shapiro & Quittner. Mr. Steinberg attended the University of Massachusetts and Boston College Law School, and has lectured on the subject of salesperson's rights at various forums.

Mr. Steinberg has written numerous case commentaries for the Uniform Commercial Code Reporter Digest. In addition, he has written several articles for continuing legal education seminars, including programs sponsored by the Practicing Law Institute and the California Business Law Institute.